The Poems of
Charles of Orleans

selected and introduced by
Sally Purcell

FYFIELD BOOKS
A CARCANET PRESS PUBLICATION

DUFOUR EDITIONS
Booksellers and Publishers
CHESTER SPRINGS, PENNA. 19425

ACKNOWLEDGEMENTS

I gratefully acknowledge here the kindness of Professor Norman Davis, F.B.A., Honorary Director of the Early English Texts Society, who permitted me to reproduce some of the text of EETS, vols. 215 and 220 (editorial notes from the latter are marked S. for Steele, and I have resolved þ and ȝ throughout into modern letters); and of Alasdair Clayre for permission to quote from his new book *Adam and the Beasts* (Faber Music).

NOTE

The line-by-line translations pretend to, and indeed have, no artistic merit; they are meant solely as a crib to help with the French text; in many cases they are inadequate because the courtly concepts are very hard to convey in modern English. In the case of the smaller poems, I have often contented myself with just glossing the difficult words, in order both to preserve the poetry and to avoid making the reader think that I *like* breaking a butterfly upon a wheel.

Several of the English poems are followed by the French and a translation into modern English, This is indicated in the title line.

SBN 902145 68 1—cloth
SBN 902145 69 X—paper

First published in 1973
by Carcanet Press Ltd
266 Councillor Lane
Cheadle Hulme, Cheadle
Cheshire SK8 5PN

Printed in Great Britain
by W & J Mackay Limited, Chatham

CONTENTS

INTRODUCTION

HAILED as a forerunner of Renaissance 'personal lyric', and vilified as a retarded representative of an already outworn and dreary manner; praised for exquisite delicacy, and reprimanded for precious trifling; compared to Petrarca, Heine, Catullus, Voltaire, Horace, Béranger, La Fontaine, Ariosto, Verlaine; treated as a perfect exponent of courtly love and chivalry, and as *un enfant au gracieux babil*—Charles d'Orléans would appear more Protean and inaccessible with every criticism one read.

My own two basic texts are—

'He is a capital example of the cultivated and refined . . . chivalry of the last chivalrous age, expert to the utmost degree in carrying out the traditional details of a graceful convention in love and literature . . . a certain easy grace and truth of expression . . . He has the urbanity of the eighteenth century without its vicious and prosaic frivolity, the poetry of the Middle Ages without their tendency to tediousness'

(Saintsbury in *Britannica*)

and—

'The question is not: to what extent is this a faithful record of an event in the poet's life? What we are concerned with is poetry, and, although light may certainly be thrown on that poetry by the author's life, temperament, and milieu, even lyric poetry is not to be judged solely in terms of autobiographical verisimilitude. In their works on mediaeval verse modern critics frequently make the mistake of looking for an allusion to a precise experience where the poet is principally concerned with writing an exercise on a set theme.'

(John Fox, *The Lyric Poetry of Charles d'Orléans*)

When Charles was young, it was possible for a high nobleman of France to offer to try by single combat with the English King the validity of the latter's claims to the French Crown; by the time he was twenty-one, Azincourt had shown how disastrous it was to fight modern wars if one's side insisted on maintaining the chivalric code; and in his old age he received nothing but unpleasantness from Louis XI, the bourgeois King who was already replacing chivalry by big business and manners by money, and who obviously considered his aged relative as a tiresome survival from a past, alien generation and way of life.

His language and the contexts that provide most of his imagery are those of feudalism, of *cortesia*, of a great noble's daily life: Summer is preceded by his 'foragers' who prepare his lodging; Charles makes 'a formal renouncement of allegiance in a parliament of love'; he goes to dwell in 'an auncient oold manar/Wherin long y had in childhod lay/Which callid is the castelle of no care'; his heart calls a grand council of his friends and clients to decide on plans for overcoming the enemy, 'Soussy, Dueil et leur aliance'; his castle *Joyeuse Plaisance* is stocked with supplies of *Confort*.

He writes within the conventions of *amour courtois* when young, emphasising the *aduersite* and *grevous lijf* of the faithful, submissive lover whose service and worship of the lady are so coolly received, living on *a praty look* that she occasionally deigns to give him; but as he grows older, and particularly after the death of his lady, he seems to outgrow the stereotyped situations, and to look more indulgently on lovers' behaviour, from a distance,

> *aha, dis je, voila des tours*
> *dont usay en mes jeunes jours.*

It would be a serious misrepresentation to read his work as an expression of his love for Bonne d'Armagnac, *or* for France, *or* for a Madame or Lady X, since it is by no means an 'anecdotal autobiography', and since it can be read with all these ideas in mind: they are all there.

As Jean-Marc Bernard says, '*Ce prince est un grand poète qui, par pudeur, recouvre d'ornements ses sentiments et ses pensées*', and, as M. Champion suggests, it is the loneliness of exile (as well perhaps as the necessity for some secrecy in expressing his private thoughts from prison) that produces such foison of allegorical personifications. '*Il a créé cette armée de petits êtres animés qui furent les différents états de sa pensée . . . autant de personnes vivantes et agissantes . . . le poète les produit dans des scènes réelles de la vie*' :* he reads the *Livre de*

* 'He has created this army of little animated beings, the various states of his own thought . . . all living, active people, whom the poet produces in settings from real life.'

Joye, but now he is old needs spectacles, *'par quoy la lettre me grossoye/. . . Pas n'avoye ceste foiblesse/Es mains de ma Dame Jeunesse'*, and this regret and gentle melancholy are conveyed with an immediate and delicate sympathy, by the peaceful familiar image. He 'once saw his heart lying unconscious in one of the dungeons, the *fosse desconfortée'* (Goodrich), and we get some slight shuddering notion of the misery endured in twenty-five years of mediaeval prisons. *'Charles a fréquenté le château de Coeur . . . il l'observera tandis qu'il entre dans sa librairie, cherchant de vieux cahiers sur son comptoir, il le surprendra écrivant des poésies sur son manuscrit illuminé de larmes . . . avec ce triste compagnon Charles traversait désolé, le jardin de sa Pensée, ce matin de mai où la gelée avait tout détruit'** (Champion), and these pictures can show the inner and the outer life intertwining more clearly than would reams of self-conscious analysis. This quality of Charles' work, this illuminating juxtaposition, appears today in songs like Alasdair Clayre's 'Irish Girl', for example—

> Once I was lonely when the frost was in the ground,
> When the birds were quiet, and streams made no sound,
> When the days rotted quickly, like fruit picked too ripe,

and 'Old Couple Walking'—

> O the willow's turning yellow and the winter smoke has gone;
> In the traffic you can hear a blackbird sing.
> It's time you and I . . .
> went out again together now it's spring.

The words and images that most readily come to a writer's mind will have an intimate sympathetic connection with his personal history, with what has happened to him in his life and with the way he has reacted; naturally the theme of prison and confinement, the figure of hermit or anchorite, the colours of black, grey, tawny and

* 'Charles has often visited Cuer's castle . . . he will watch him entering his library, to look out some old account-books on his desk, he will surprise him writing poems in his manuscript book illuminated with tears . . . with this sad companion Charles miserably walked through the garden of his Thought, on that May morning when the frost had destroyed everything there.'

vert perdu (standing for mourning, melancholy, constancy in sadness) recur with some frequency and cumulative effect in Charles' poems. Naturally the theme of death is most prominent in the English poems, in particular those with no known French equivalent. His work is full of loneliness, exile, wandering in the forest alone, of silence and retreat as self-preservation—

> *Quelque chose derriere*
> *Couvient tousjours garder,*
> *On ne peut pas monstrer*
> *Sa voulenté entiere.*

(beginning of rondeau LXVII).

Cigada suggests that this attitude of 'spiritual evasiveness' was natural to Charles, that he always preferred to keep himself and his real feelings out of the direct light, and that this tendency could not but have been made more emphatic by his long captivity. In rondeau CLI, he counsels himself: 'Think henceforward of yourself, and care but little for the rest. I see this world growing steadily worse; henceforward think of yourself. Watch and hear, but speak not much; Almighty God will act as he will; look to yourself.'

> *Pense de toy*
> *Dorenavant,*
> *Du demourant*
> *Te chaille poy.*
>
> *Ce monde voy*
> *En enpirant,*
> *Pense de toy*
> *Dorenavant.*
>
> *Regarde et oy,*
> *Va peu parlant;*
> *Dieu tout puissant*
> *Fera de soy;*
> *Pense de toy.*

The favourite mediaeval theme of the transitory nature of this world and all its beauty is handled by Charles with a rare delicacy and fastidiousness; in his ballad of dead ladies he shows no trace of the common tendency to dwell on the processes of death and decay, but rather a gentle melancholy, *'en pleurant tendrement'*. He concludes, as the genre demands, 'that this world nys but even a thyng in vayne', but turns even this into graceful courtly wit by saying that Death must be trying to destroy all Delight and 'worldly plesere' by stealing so many fair ladies from the world, since truly, without them, 'mafay, . . . this world nys but even a thyng in vayne'. You would not find Villon doing that; he is a great deal more outspoken, about the symptoms of approaching death, the fate of hanged men's bodies, the lesson of perfect equality the charnel-house teaches. Nor would you find in his work such effects as—

> Ther nys leef nor flowre that doth endewre
> But a sesoun as sowne doth in a belle.

I do not intend to pronounce any judgement about the relative merits of Charles and Villon; I agree for once with Bullrich when he says that the difference between the two is so great that the best course is to abstain from playing off one against the other. We know that the two men met; we know that Villon wrote *'O louee concepcion'* and *'Combien que j'ay leu en ung dit'* (whether these form one poem or two) for the birth (19 December 1457) or the triumphal entry into Orleans (17 July 1460) of Charles' daughter Marie, and that Villon took part in the *'débat de la fontaine'* or *'concours de Blois'*, which took place between December 1457 and 1460. Villon's contribution to the latter is copied into Charles' personal manuscript, probably not by Villon himself, but perhaps copied by someone else from his autograph. Since he does not figure any further in Charles' *liber amicorum*, one feels he may have been given a polite dismissal for pinching the spoons, but this must remain in the realms of romantic conjecture, I fear.

THE FRENCH poems are preserved in Charles' personal MS, B.N. fr. 25458, and in a number of others more or less derived from it. Originally in 25458 Charles had left blanks on various pages for the music, so that the *chanson* or *rondeau* was on the lower half of the page, but later on these gaps were filled up by other scribes with assorted rondeaux, out of order. This arrangement is followed by MSS deriving from 25458, but not by Grenoble 873, copied from it between 1461 and 1464/5 by the Duke's Latin secretary Astezan; it contains translations into Latin of all Charles' pre-1453 poems preserved in his own book, but its main value is in the help it affords for establishing their order. MS Carpentras 375, made for Marie de Clèves *c.* 1455–8, is mechanically copied from 25458, but some of its transcriptions were made before the latter underwent corrections and alterations, so that we have some control over these. The post-1456 part of Carpentras is a kind of *journal poétique* in different hands, a *mise au courant* of the Duke's latest works, taken presumably from his own MS, and a collection of friends' poems, poems exchanged with other courtly writers such as King René, and poems written for competitions, like the famous set that all begin '*Je meurs de soif auprès de la fontaine*'—the whole comprising what used to be called a *liber amicorum*. MS B.N. fr. 1104, that used by the Abbé Sallier when resurrecting Charles' poetry in 1734, is a copy of Charles' own MS, executed between 1458 and 1465 and following the already-confused order of 25458. B. M. Harley 6916 is a copy of B.N. fr. 25458, made not long after it.

Steele points out the close similarity in shape, form, layout and order of poems between 25458 and B. M. Harley 682, which contains Charles' English poems (at least half of them having no French original, by the way), which would suggest a common origin, dating perhaps from the poet's residence in England. The English is not a mere translation or imitation, but the differences in treatment are imposed by the differences between the two languages ('the diffuseness of the English compared with the concise elegance of the French'), and between their respective readiness to take poetry (the French tradition being older and more fully developed). The French *ballades* are often more polished re-workings of the English. 'The nature of the variations between the French and English poems, where they contrast, is dead against the idea of their being due to a translator'; the corrections and alterations are those of an author, and that author one acquainted with both Charles' unpublished work and the secret correspondence in *ballades* between Charles and Burgundy; the partisans of an anonymous translator have no name to put forward, no idea why he did not translate the French more closely, and no explanation why he should have bothered, at a time when most educated people spoke French and read it adequately, to make his translation at all. Although Continental critical opinion seems to be that Charles could not possibly have written these poems, but that anyone else could, and that there is very little interest anyway in naming the Anon., one may conclude with Steele that 'up to now a purely unfounded prejudice has deprived him of the honours of his English verse'.

John Fox in *Romania 86* disposes of the mythical translator whose work is *'sans intérêt pour une étude de Charles'*, in a closely-reasoned and sensible article; he points out that the relationship between the French and English texts is often much too tenuous for one to be called a translation of the other—at the most, one might be called a re-handling or adaptation of the other—and that there is often nothing to show which came first. The English ballads without French equivalents are probably quite independent poems, and it is to be noted that as the collection proceeds the English poems become more loosely attached to the French—that is, as Charles acquires a better knowledge of his forcibly adopted language. That he was considered very proficient in English is evident from Duke Humphrey's objection to his proposed release, that he was too 'subtle' and had found out far too much about English policy and the true inner state of the country, to be allowed to use this knowledge for France's benefit.

Fox examines many intentional changes in the texts which can have nothing to do with the hypothetical incompetence of a translator, and remarks that Charles seems often to have been concerned with correspondence of sound rather than of sense: *'non pas maladresse et tâtonnements, mais expériences et exploitation des capacités acoustiques et rhythmiques des deux langues'.** He quotes (Steele, ll. 3085–7) lines which would sound very silly from a translator—

> But where y fayle y pray yow hertily
> That rede my werk and kan doon bet than y
> Where as y fayle ye lust amende hit ay.

Until 1959, Charles' only known religious poem was a *carole* in

* 'not clumsiness and groping, but experiments and exploitation of the acoustic and rhythmic capabilities of the two languages.'

Latin, published by M. Champion; but in this year it was discovered that MS. B.N. lat. 1203, which is largely in his autograph, contained the rough draft of a long poem in monorhymed quatrains, the *'Canticum Amoris'*, which is neatly transcribed by one of his English scribes in B.N. lat. 1196. It was written after the death of his second wife, Bonne, who had been living since 1415 with her mother as a recluse in the convent of the Cordeliers at Rodez; she was buried, in the Franciscan habit, some time after 1430.

Charles was a frequent visitor to the London Greyfriars, whose library had been founded by his spiritual director Thomas Wynchelsey, author of an *Instructorium providi peregrini* dedicated to Charles, and like all lettered men of his time he was bilingual, naturally using Latin for sacred and the vernacular for profane matters; he and his brother Angoulême read and copied many Franciscan works of devotion, such as Pseudo-Bonaventura's *Stimulus Amoris*, during their captivity, composed their own Latin prayers and copied out others, in B.N. lat. 1203, which an inventory characterises as *'un livret en papier escrit de la main de mondit seigneur, contenant plusieurs oroisons'*.

The poem treats of God's immense bounty and goodness, and of all the reasons for which the soul should love God: it describes the spring—

> *Ecce ligni genera multa procreantur,*
> *Fronde, flore, fructibus mire decorantur;*
> *Agri multa seminum fruge fecundantur,*
> *Variis graminibus cespites ornantur,*
> *Floribus multimodis prata purpurantur.*
> *. . . Sed in hiis diligere disce Creatorem.*

It considers the Incarnation as the greatest proof of God's love for man, a theme also handled in the Latin *carole*—

> *Quam miranda caritas Dei comprobatur,*
> *Cum amoris gracia Deus incarnatur.*

The poet pictures the brilliant ranks of heaven (*'Mens percurrens lucidas celi mansiones'*), and urges his soul to consider the virtues that have won its inhabitants their place there—

> *Quociens te senseris, anima, tristari,*
> *Martirum constanciam discas imitari,*

begging for the favour of their prayers and the benefits of their merits (*'Horumque suffragia constanter implora'*).

In a moving passage he describes the pomps of this world as he had known them, and reminds himself that the soul must not attach itself to such transitory and hollow pleasures, but to God the source of true good—

> *Cum regalis curie festa celebrantur,*
> *Et preclaris milites stolis decorantur,*
> *Dominarum agmina gemmis perornantur,*
> *Multi visu talium mire delectantur. . . .*
> *Anima heu misera, cur infatuaris*
> *Ut quid transitoriis usquam delectaris?*
> *Nonne cum doloribus transeunt amaris*
> *Cuncta temporalia quibus jocundaris?*

A SIMPLIFIED family tree may be in order here, to explain Charles' connections and his political importance—

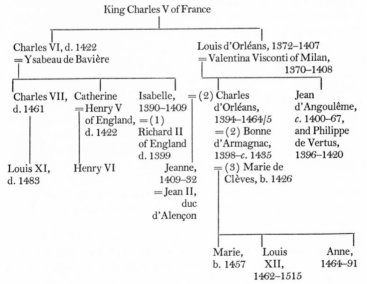

King Charles V of France

Charles VI, d. 1422
= Ysabeau de Bavière

Louis d'Orléans, 1372–1407
= Valentina Visconti of Milan, 1370–1408

Charles VII, d. 1461

Catherine
= Henry V of England, d. 1422

Isabelle, 1390–1409
= (1) Richard II of England d. 1399

= (2) Charles d'Orléans, 1394–1464/5
= (2) Bonne d'Armagnac, 1398–c. 1435
= (3) Marie de Clèves, b. 1426

Jean d'Angoulême, c. 1400–67, and Philippe de Vertus, 1396–1420

Louis XI, d. 1483

Henry VI

Jeanne, 1409–32
= Jean II, duc d'Alençon

Marie, b. 1457

Louis XII, 1462–1515

Anne, 1464–91

15

The point must be made that by the Treaty of Troyes of 1420 Charles VI promised to let Henry V have the French Crown at his death, and disinherited his one remaining son, the sickly Charles de Ponthieu, whom Jeanne d'Arc later crowned King; Henry realised that if this young man died, the next legal and rightful heir was the imprisoned Charles d'Orléans. Henry died on 31 August 1422, and Charles VI on 21 October 1422, leaving the Crowns of both kingdoms to the nine-month-old Henry VI.

Born at Paris on 24 November 1394, Charles was the eldest surviving son of the mad King's only brother, and hence a very important individual; in 1406 he was married to his cousin Isabelle de France. She had been married at the age of seven to King Richard II of England, and after his murder the English had retained the child widow in their custody, being understandably reluctant to restore her dowry to France. When she was handed back and married to Charles, it seems that Isabelle was most chagrined at having to lose her title of Queen, and throughout the wedding ceremony, says the chronicler, *'pleuroit fort la dite Isabelle'*.

On 23 November 1407 Charles abruptly became the head of his house and of the Armagnac-Orléans political faction, on the assassination of his father by their enemy Burgundy; Louis had been riding away from the Queen's house by the Porte Barbette that evening (it was widely supposed that they were lovers), when he was struck down and almost literally hacked to pieces by hired knife-men. Charles' first duty was to avenge the murder and to rehabilitate his father's character against the assiduous slanders Burgundy was spreading to justify his crime; indeed, he had hired one Maître Jean Petit from the Sorbonne to preach publicly in Paris that the late duc d'Orléans had been so unspeakably vile that the country owed a debt of gratitude to Jean Sans-Peur for having removed him. Charles adopted deep mourning for all public appearances, and his mother Valentine took the motto '*Riens ne m'est plus, plus ne m'est rien*', with the touching device of the *chantepleure*, the little water-sprinkler that signifies her never-ceasing tears, which was later assumed in her memory by Charles' third wife Marie.

Valentine died on 4 December 1408, worn out by her tireless efforts to obtain justice from the royal court, and on 13 September of the following year Isabelle died in childbirth, leaving a daughter, Jeanne.

Father, widower, figurehead of a large political faction, duc d'Orléans and committed to continuing a vendetta, in 1410 at the age of fifteen Charles married Bonne d'Armagnac, third child of Bernard VII, comte d'Armagnac, who was nearly twelve, in order to confirm his alliance with the Armagnacs and to enable himself to revenge his father; he marched on Paris with his army in the following year, while Jean Sans-Peur of Burgundy was raising the butchers' revolt, terrorising the capital and calling in the English *godons* as his allies. At the same time, he signed a contract of marriage between his daughter (aged nine months) and the six-year-old Jean, duc d'Alençon, later companion in arms to St. Jeanne d'Arc.

He was defeated, put to flight and excommunicated for his defiance of Burgundy, to be reconciled and restored in 1412; he achieved the rehabilitation of his father and the condemnation of Burgundy in 1414; and after Azincourt, his first engagement (25 October 1415), he was picked out from under a heap of dead and taken prisoner. Reaching England shortly before his twenty-first birthday, paraded through the streets and at Canterbury taken to a service of thanksgiving for his own defeat, he joined his brother Jean d'Angoulême, who had been a hostage there since 1412, and began negotiations about ransom. He was kept in various prisons, in the Tower (where he was a contemporary of the poet James I of Scotland), Pontefract (where Richard II had been murdered), Fotheringay, Ampthill (in the custody of Sir John Cornwall, Henry IV's brother-in-law), Windsor—and all the time was trying to raise the enormous ransom money demanded from his depleted and ravaged estates in France. Virtually everything he or his brother wanted could be brought from their estates—at a price, and through a long and tedious machinery of safe-conducts and customs permission that sounds quite modern in its awkwardness. The English were guilty of bad faith, hypocrisy and downright greed to an extraordinary degree—M. Dupont-Ferrier has examined the captivity of Jean d'Angoulême in the light of the ideas then prevailing that prisoners were a useful source of revenue, objects to be sold to the highest bidder or left in one's will, and shows up the abominable rapacity of the Clarences and Somersets in their custody of these profitable unfortunates. Many of the Orléans heirlooms were sold to keep these predators at bay; one particularly rich jewelled gold 'garland' was lost for ever because the noble lady then benefiting from Charles' imprisonment was not satisfied by the first two valuations that had been made, so sent it for a more expert valuation to a banker at Genoa, on the way to whom it simply disappeared.

On 10 September 1419 Jean Sans-Peur was treacherously murdered; in 1420 Charles' brother Philippe de Vertus, who had been managing his estates, died, and the responsibilities of head of the family fell on their bastard half-brother Dunois. In France appeared a *'Pucelle nommée Jehanne, que Dieu mouvoit'*, who had many revelations concerning Charles, and planned to come to England to rescue him; at her trial she was to declare *'que Dieu aime bien le duc d'Orléans, et qu'elle avoit eu plus de révélations de lui que d'homme de France, excepté de son roy.'*[*]

But the Maid went to the stake in 1431, and Bonne d'Armagnac died in 1435 or thereabouts, and still the brothers remained in prison. They learned English (Jean d'Angoulême had a *Canterbury Tales* copied for him and annotated it); they both composed prayers, read Boethius and modern works of piety; Charles wrote poems, and perhaps his brother did too.

His constant offers of help as mediator in peace conferences were sometimes accepted, but never carried much further; the authorities feared that he knew too much about England, were well aware of his dynastic importance, and had been recommended by Henry V's will not to let him go until Henry VI should attain his majority. By the efforts of Philippe, the new Duke of Burgundy, and of his Duchess (daugher of Henry IV's sister Philippa, and a zealous worker for peace between France and England), Charles was eventually freed in 1440, and had to thank the son of his father's murderer publicly. He married Burgundy's niece Marie de Clèves, who was fourteen, and spent the next five years working for peace between England, France, and Burgundy, and for his brother's release (1445).

After an abortive expedition to reclaim the town of Asti, which he inherited from his mother, from the usurping Sforza, in 1447, he settled down to a tranquil and premature old age (in 1433 he had told French visitors that he was *'en bon point de corps, en desplaisance*

[*] 'that God loves well the Duke of Orleans, and that she had had more revelations concerning him than of any other man in France, but her King.'

de ce qu'il usoit le meilleur temps de son eage prisonnier') at his court of Blois, devoting himself mainly to books, chess, music, and the literary competitions he held for visiting poets. He emerged into public life again in 1458, to defend his son-in-law Alençon against a charge of treason (although Jeanne d'Orléans had died in 1432 and Alençon had married again, he and Charles had always remained on very close terms, perhaps because Charles had no son), in a speech which is preserved in M.S B.N. fr. 1104. Alençon was condemned to death, but saved by the intervention of Arthur, duc de Bretagne.

Charles' daughter Marie, whose birth or triumphal entry into Orléans is celebrated by Villon, was born on 19 December 1457; his son, who was to become Louis XII, on 27 June 1462; and his daughter Anne, who took the veil in 1478 and died as Abbess of Fontevrault in 1491, was the last of his children, born in 1464.

In 1461 the old duke acted as chief mourner at the funeral of Charles VII, and it is probable that about this time he stopped writing; the latest poem we can date is the rondeau of farewell, *'Salués moy toute la compaignie'*, composed perhaps in late 1461. And he died at Amboise on his way home on 4/5 January 1464/5.

A NOTE ON ALLEGORY

First, the O.E.D. defines allegory as: '1. Description of a subject under the guise of some other subject of aptly suggestive resemblance', and quotes from Wyclif in 1382, 'allegorie, or goostly undirstondinge', and from Puttenham in 1589, 'Properly and in his principall vertue Allegoria is when we do speake in sence translatiue and wrested from the owne signification, neuerthelesse applied to another not altogether contrary, but hauing much conueniencie with it'; next it gives: '2. An instance of such description; a figurative sentence, discourse, or narrative, in which properties and circumstances attributed to the apparent subject really refer to the subject they are meant to suggest; an extended or continued metaphor'; and it derives the word from ἀλληγορία, literally 'speaking otherwise than one seems to speak'.

Large areas of mediaeval thought and poetry will remain in-
* 'in good shape physically, in discontent that he was using up the best part of his life in prison.'

explicably barren, ugly, or inaccessible to us if we ignore or misunderstand their allegories; the knowledge that tapestries showing faded figures courteously posturing represent, say, *Dangier* banished by *Liesse* and *Bel-Acueil*, leaves us cold.

To mediaeval thought these 'extended or continued metaphors' and personifications are not just a pleasant game; they are part of a great, elaborate, comprehensive pattern. Everything in the created world is capable of a symbolic interpretation, not merely an arbitrary one depending on the observer's wit, but an intrinsic one intended and 'built-in' by the Creator for our better understanding. In bestiaries, the salamander can live in fire and feed upon it without harm; God has caused this to be so, that we may see in the creature the type of the good Christian soul existing in a naughty world; the lion's offspring are born dead and he resurrects them by his powerful roaring after three days, and God designed this, not merely (in fact hardly at all) for our better knowledge of the lion, but in order that we might see in the fact (for as such it was unquestioningly accepted) a type of the Son's resurrection at His Father's summons.

Similarly, what we should call 'abstractions', like the Seven Liberal Arts or the Four Cardinal Virtues, may be figured as ladies bearing appropriately symbolic objects (Temperance with a bridle, Justice with sword and scales, Grammar with a schoolmaster's birch, for instance), or by the objects alone. A bridle can *mean* temperance and self-control just as much as it *means* its practical function as a piece of harness. Saints are represented either *with* or *by* their emblems, St. Catherine's wheel, St. Laurence's gridiron, and so forth, the object recalling in a single compressed statement the saint's history, and in particular his martyrdom. We still say that 'the Crown' owns or does something, meaning both the individual Sovereign and the permanent concept of the powers and qualities which are at the moment embodied in him.

The detailed personification of such apparently intractable concepts as Nature, Wisdom, the World-Soul, by serious authors like Bernard Silvestris, the twelfth-century Platonist, and Alanus de Insulis, may bewilder us now that we are unaccustomed to visualise ideas in this way; but religious dogma, philosophical speculation, and complicated psychological analysis can in fact be expressed with great accuracy and concision through allegory.

Charles handles allegory with great skill, subtlety and precision. One of his chief characters is *Cuer*, the personification of his own heart, with whom he holds long conversations, not as a whimsical or precious game, but as a means of representing complicated states of mind. Fortunately he had no modern psychological jargon available to him, and so he presents us with, for example, the immediately effective picture of Heart lying in a foul dungeon, alone and neglected, *'en la fosse desconfortée'* or an account of his conversation with Heart, persuading him in vain to give up a profitless, inexplicable and painful love—*'si lui dis je que c'est folie'*. Heart has withdrawn from the world and become a hermit, 'in the hermitage of Thought'. (*Pensee* in Charles' language denotes an abstracted in-turned melancholy state, into which the lover frequently falls), since Fortune and Sadness have banished him from Delight. He has nowhere to dwell but the wood of Melancholy, and is content to remain there, although the poet tells him this is folly. He persists in this life, he is governed by the counsels of Distress who is constantly advising him, and despite all the poet's arguments, he keeps to his folly. Charles advises his lady to write to Heart and dissuade him from the vows he has taken as hermit (to renounce the riches of Pleasure and Sweet Thought, and to wear the garb of Unhappiness all his life); Heart will take no comfort from anything anyone says to him, and the lady is the only person he will listen to.

In one rondeau, Heart is found seated between Comfort and Grief; in another, he lies in the prisons of *Pensee*; one day Charles comes upon him writing 'the true story of grief' in his book of *Pensee*; one night he keeps Charles awake by staying up to read *ou rommant de Plaisant Penser* and asking him to listen (at that time, most people who could read still did so more or less aloud). In ballade 37 Heart wears black, as for many years Charles did on all public occasions in mourning for his murdered and as yet unavenged father.

In ballade 97, Heart is an accountant or steward who reports to Charles on the state of his finances; the poet asks whether he has made any saving during the time he has been serving Love, and Heart replies that he must first consult his papers; he looks out several old ledgers in his office, and brings back the relevant book to his master, tots up the figures and regretfully concludes that although some profit might have been expected, none has actually been made.

In the following ballade, Charles, Heart and *Penser* are sailing from Orleans to Blois, leaning over the side and watching the other ships, that sail lightly since they have *'a plaisir et a gré le vent'*; Heart wishes he had their good fortune, so that he might spread the sail of Comfort to a favourable wind—but as it is, whenever he travels in the boat of the World, the water of Fortune is so still that without the aid of Hope's oars he would never move forward at all. Charles watches the boats go up river, as he himself descends *'contre les vagues de Tourment'*, hoping that in God's good time a favourable wind will come for him. In this poem the allegory is handled with such skill and lightness of touch that we feel no surprise when one allegorical personification creates a further dimension by using in an allegorical speech images derived from the opening setting in the real world—an unusual and very satisfying device of pattern.

There are plenty more images of *Cuer*: Charles the sovereign summons the Three Estates of his heart in order to take counsel of them; Painful News (of his lady's illness) so affects *Cuer* that he longs to die, 'and says he is aweary of his life'; he is wounded by Pleasant Beauty, so severely that he falls into the fever of Love; and so on.

Charles uses many images from everyday life with allegorical application; I refer to a handful here for example's sake, and painstakingly full analyses can be found in Goodrich. He keeps in the treasury of his thought a mirror sold to him by Love; he plays chess with *Faulx Dangier* in the presence of Love, and loses in the end when Fortune comes to help his opponent; Fortune exiles him to the forest of Wearisome Sadness; at his lady's funeral the service is sung by Grievous Thought, the candles are of Pitiful Sighs, and the tomb is made all of Regrets painted with tears; on a journey he sends his *fourriers* ahead to prepare his lodging in the city of Destiny; Hope loads the ship of Good News with a cargo of Comfort, and it is to sail from France over the sea of Fortune to the harbour of Desire. Charles, in his old age, *'quant je lis ou livre de Joye,/ Les lunettes prens pour le mieulx,/Par quoy la lettre me grossoye'* (he cannot read the book of Joy as plainly as he used, and has to wear spectacles now, a weakness he never knew 'in the hands of Madame Jeunesse'.) A device common to most other writers of allegory, that of making a personification offspring, parent, spouse or sibling of another, is very seldom found in Charles' work, and although I do not pretend to be a psychological critic, I think that his personal life is not without relevance here.

Although it would be possible to write many thousands of words listing other allegorical figures and objects Charles uses, I shall conclude with an examination of the important concept *Nonchaloir*, which Dom Harold Watson calls 'the key word and attitude of his maturity', and of the guises it assumes. The word may mean 'nonchalance, apathy, inaction, indifference, negligence, lack of curiosity', and in Charles' work comes to mean a voluntary indifference,' a sort of sentimental retreat' made in self-defence against unhappiness, painful memories, and the sufferings of love. *Nonchaloir* is his protector, his doctor (who takes his pulse and prescribes more rest and sleep), the remedy (*emplastre*) that he applies to his heart to cure it of the sickness of love, a narcotic or sedative perhaps originally intended to dull the pains of homesickness and exile, a hermitage where he can take refuge from *Ennui*.

In the '*Songe en Complainte*', when he has received his honourable discharge from Love's service, he is led by Comfort to the ancient manor-house where he lived in childhood, '*que l'en appelle Nonchaloir*'; he is received by *Passe Temps*, the 'governor' of the house, who allows him to take up residence there for the rest of his life. Charles writes an elegant verse letter to Love, 'Prince of worldly sweetness', thanking him for these favours, and ending with the standard epistolary formulae of date, place, and signature—

> *Escript ce jour troisiesme, vers le soir,*
> *En novembre, ou lieu de Nonchaloir,*
> *Le bien vostre, Charles, duc d'Orlians,*
> *Qui jadis fu l'un de voz vrais servans.*

If one compares Charles' skilful and sensitive allegory with the work of less gifted users of the device, such as his friend King René de Sicile, whose long and convoluted *Livre du Cuer d'Amours esprins* came out in late 1457, it will appear that Charles was so temperamentally suited to this mode of expression as to make of it his personal style and to achieve in it effects of unsurpassed elegance, pathos, or subtlety. By nature, as M. Bernard points out, he was led by modesty and delicacy to veil his feelings in image and metaphor; during his captivity, twenty-five years of constraint and anxiety almost impossible for us to imagine, he must have found it politic to cover in this way ideas whose open expression could be dangerous; and symbolic and allegorical interpretation of the whole surrounding world was still a living and creative way of thought. By making the effort of imaginative sympathy in this direction, we may be able to understand a little more *'le moyen âge énorme et délicat'*, and incidentally to appreciate some very fine poetry.

COMPARISON of the Steele and Champion editions, of the English and the French poems, from MSS Harley 682 and B.N. fr. 25458 respectively:

La Retenue d'Amours	English ll. 1–202 (the first quire of *c.* 400 lines is missing)
Ballades I–LVII	Ballades 1–57
—	,, 58–60
LVIII	,, 61
—	,, 62
LIX–LXX	,, 63–72
—	,, 73
Songe en Complainte, and ballades continuing its story i–vii	Vision in Complaint, followed by ballades 74–81; ends 13th. Nov. 1437.
Ballades LXXIII,	Ballade 82
LXXII	83

Love's Renewal, beginning with a long allegorical narrative poem, takes up the story where the above cycle leaves it, at the poet's release from Love's service after the death of his lady. Explains how he was persuaded to take a new lady.

only four of these exist in the French, Ballades 107, 101, 111, 113; as English poems, they 'come from the French and from originals to which no one but Orléans himself could have had access' (Goodrich), e.g. the letter-poem to Burgundy and the re-writing of Burgundy's answer.

Ballades 85–121; ends with Charles' release in 1440.

No ballade; songs I–LII

Ballade 84, introducing a collection of songs; 1–52 are in the French also, 53–102 exist only in English.

songs LIII–LXXXIX exist only in French.

One quire, containing rondels 72–86 inclusive, is lost.

Then come three *caroles* in French with English counterparts, and one *carole* in Latin and five in English only.

five complaintes in French

only no. iii occurs in English

One letter and two miscellaneous poems.

Rondeaux I–CCCCXXXV, Vol. II of Champion.

Not long a-goo y hyed me apase
In secret wise myn hert forto counsayle
Himsilf forto withdrawe as for a space
Out of louys paynfulle thought and trauayle
To which he seide me nay sett there a nayle
Speke me no more therof y hertly pray
For god wot to loue y shalle me payne
For y haue chose the fayrist that be may
As me reportid hath myn eyen twayne

Now pardone me y seide as in this case
Forwhi y say hit for oure bothe avayle
With alle the power that god welle in me hase
That in good trouthe thou dost me to mervayle
Seest thou not welle that fortune doth vs fayle
Hast thou good lust to lyue in sorow/nay
I-wis he seide y trust more to attayne
I had a praty look yit yestirday
As me reportid hath myn eyen twayne

Allas seide y thou fonnyst as haue y grace
That for oon look thi lijf lust to biwayle
For countenaunce or lookis of hir face
Knowist thou hir thought/ye cast me lo a kayle

lines 5f. 'Mais il me dist bien fellement (bitterly, harshly)/"Ne m'en parlez plus, je vous prie".'
sett there a nayle, hold there, go no further.
in verse 2, the poet answers, 'Vueilliez me pardoner,/Car je vous jure mon serement/Que conseil vous cuide (mean) donner,/A mon povair, tresloyaument;/Voulez vous sans allegement/En doleur finer vostre vie?'
god welle, good will.
fonnyst, are being foolish.
ye cast me lo a kayle; S. says 'well then, throw me down a skittle', meaning 'you are talking nonsense'. I suggest that it may mean 'go

O pese/quod he now good y lust not rayle
Nor y bileue no word thou dost me say
For trewly serue y shalle and neuyr fayne
Of good which is the best/leue this aray
As me reportid hath myn eyen twayne

O y-wis madame in this maner aray
Myn hert and y thus haue ye brost atwayne
But what swete hert as gide vs such a way
As me reportid hath myn eyen twayne

on then, just try; have a go and see how close you get to the mark
(to the truth)'. No equivalent in the French.
rayle, joke.
atwayne, apart (literally, in two).
No envoy in the French.

When y am leyd to slepe as for a stound
To haue my rest y kan in no manere
For alle the nyght myn hert aredith round
As in the romaunce of plesaunt pancer
Me praiyng so as him to hark and here
And y ne dar his loue disobay
In dowtyng so to do him displesere
This is my slepe y-falle into decay

In this book which he redde is write & bound
As alle dedis of my lady dere
Which doth myn hert in laughter oft abound
When he hit rett or tellith the matere
Which gretly is to prayse without were
For y my silf delite it here mafay
Which if thei herde so wolde eche straungere
This is my slepe y-falle into decay

As with myn eyen a respit to be found
As for an howre y axe not for a yere
For which dispite welnygh he doth confounde
That they ne kan fulfille my desere
For which to rage and sighe as in a gere
He farith so that even as welle y may
As make him stynt likke out a cole of fyre
This is my slepe y-falle into decay

pancer is the equivalent of *penser*, 'thought'; Watson Taylor hope-
fully reads *chaucer*!
line 6, *loue* is crossed out and *welle* (= will) written in the margin.
dowtyng, fearing.
rett, reads.
were (in line 13), doubt.
delite it here mafay, takes delight in hearing it, by my faith.
gere, capricious mood, S.
stynt, stop, calm down.

Thus may y loo more souner wyn my bere
Then make my froward hert to me obay
For with myn hurt he doth him silf achere
This is my slepe y-falle into dacay

bere, tomb, bier.

Quant je suis couschié en mon lit,
Je ne puis en paix reposer;
Car toute la nuit mon cueur lit
Ou rommant de Plaisant Penser,
Et me prie de l'escouter.
Si ne l'ose desobeir
Pour doubte de le courroucer;
Ainsi je laisse le dormir.

Ce livre si est tout escript
Des fais de ma Dame sans per;
Souvent mon cueur de joye rit,
Quand il les list ou oyt compter;
Car certes tant sont a louer
Qu'il y prent souverain plaisir;
Moy mesmes ne m'en puis lasser,
Ainsi je laisse le dormir.

Se mes yeulx demandent respit
Par Sommeil qui les vient grever,
Il les tense par grant despit,
Et si ne les peut surmonter;
Il ne cesse de soupirer
A part soy; j'ay lors, sans mentir,
Grant paine de le rapaiser,
Ainsi je laisse le dormir.

Amour, je ne puis gouverner
Mon cueur; car tant vous veult servir
Qu'il ne scet jour ne nuit cesser;
Ainsi je laisse le dormir.

When I am laid in my bed,
I cannot rest in peace;
For all night long my heart reads
(In) the romance of Pleasant Thought,
And asks me to listen.
And I dare not disobey him
For fear of angering him;
So I leave my sleeping.

This book is all written
Of the deeds of my peerless Lady;
Often my heart laughs for joy
When he reads them or hears them told;
For certainly they are so much to be praised
That he takes therein supreme pleasure;
And I myself cannot tire of them,
And so I leave my sleeping.

If my eyes ask for some respite
Through Sleep that weighs upon them,
He reprimands them in great despite,
And yet he cannot overcome them;
He never stops sighing
Privately to himself, and then, I tell no lie, I have
Great difficulty in appeasing him,
And so I leave my sleeping.

O Love, I cannot govern
My heart, for he wishes so much to serve you
That he knows not how to stop, night or day;
And so I leave my sleeping.

Now what tidyng my lady & mastres
How farith oure loue y pray yow hertily
For in my side y make yow sewre promys
In oon purpos that y me kepe trewly
Without contrary thought in my party
Which is that y shalle serue yow to my last
As only yowre wherfore as wot ye how
As in yowre part now be not childisshe gast
But in liche wise let se aquytith yow

Al be that daunger hath and gret distres
As of long tyme soiournyd alle to nygh
Mi nakid hert thorugh force of hir rewdenes
Of turnys straunge him shewyng fulle many
Allas they shulde so haue ther dwellyng fy
In louys court/but pite slepith fast
Yet y shalle do my part in what y mowe
As with my trouthe him forto ouyrcast
But in liche wise lete se aquytith yow

For though the ennoy of payne and heuynes
long time hath had ther course bi gret maystry
Yet in the lusty sesoun of gladnes
Wolle come my socoure truste y verily
Vnto oure hertis bothe/for wot ye whi

gast, frightened. Not in the French.
rewdenes, harshness, S.
lines 10ff. 'Combien que Dangier et Destresse/Ont fait longuement
leurs sejours/Avec mon cueur, et par rudesse/Luy ont moustré
d'estranges tours . . .'
lines 16f. 'Si mettray paine que briefment/Loyaulté sur eulx ait
maistrie'.
mowe, may.
lines 19ff. 'Quoyque la nue (cloud) de Tristesse/Par un long temps
ait fait son cours,/Aprés le beau temps de Lyesse/Vendra . . .'
lines 24f. 'mon recours/J'ay en Espoir, en qui me fie,/Et en vous,
Belle, seulement'.

Yet haue y hope as y had tyme a-past
Saue only yow/which y most truste now
For where my mynde is sayle ye ar the mast
But in liche wise let se aquytith yow

Let me not goon as oon vnknowe vnbast
For yowre y am as y haue made a vow
That knowist thou lord/to knowe that power hast
But in liche wise let se aquytith yow

line 26 not in the French at all.
vnbast, unkissed.
envoy. 'Soiés seure, ma doulce amie,
      Que je vous ayme loyaument.
      Or, vous requier et vous supplie,
      Acquittiez vous pareillement.'

Honure and prays as mot to him habound
That first did fynde the wayes of writyng
For comfort gret ordeynyd he that stounde
To suche as haue of louys payne felyng
For when to speke they naue tyme nor metyng
To say ther ladies of ther aduersite
Yet doth it them a gret tranquyllite
Forto endite and sende as in writyng
What grevous lijf they lede as semeth me
Only for loue and feithfulle trewe servyng

Who so that write how he is wrappid & wounde
In suche greef as kan kepe him from laughyng
And so may sende it to his lady round
Which is the leche to alle his soore felyng
If then to rede hit be to her plesyng
She may right welle therin perceyue and se
What woofulle gouernaunce endewrith he
Of whiche pite may geue her hit mevyng
That his desert is reward of mercy
Only for loue and feithfulle trewe servyng

That hit is thus in myn hert haue y found
And knowe the craft for when he tath sekyng
No thyng kan him appese vpon the ground
To he haue send or made sum endityng
On the fayre which is his most likyng
Of which if so that his fortune be

that stounde, at that time.
line 4. 'Pour amans qui sont en martire'.
line 12. 'Son dueil, qui trop le tient de rire'.
round, right away; 'au plus tost'.
leche, physician.
tath sekyng, begins to sigh; 'quant il souspire'.
line 25. 'Vers la belle que tant desire'.

34

To haue a response of hir gret bounte
He tath therin so huge a reioysyng
That forget is he had on his party
Only for loue and feithfulle trewe servyng

But what madame crist ewre me so that ye
May vndirstonde as bi my mouth telyng
What y haue dewrid in tymys quantite
Only for loue and feithfulle trewe servyng

lines 27f. 'Oïr nouvelles seulement/De sa doulce beauté sans per',
i.e. in the French the heart is content if he only hears some news
of the lady.
envoy. 'Ma Dame, Dieu doint que briefment
          Vous puisse de bouche compter
          Ce que j'ay souffert longuement
          Pour bien et loyaument amer!'
ewre, grant.

Mon cueur a envoyé querir
Tous ses bien vueillans et amis,
Il veult son grant conseil tenir
Avec eulx, pour avoir advis
Comment pourra ses ennemis,
Soussy, Dueil et leur aliance,
Surmonter et tost deconfire,
Qui desirent de le destruire
En la prison de Desplaisance.

En desert ont mis son plaisir,
Et joye tenu en pastis;
Mais Confort lui a, sans faillir,
De nouvel loyaument promis
Qu'ilz seront deffais et bannis;
De ce se fait fort Esperance,
Et plus avant que n'ose dire;
C'est ce qui estaint son martire
En la prison de Desplaisance.

Briefment voye le temps venir,
J'en prie a Dieu de paradis,
Que chascun puist vers son desir
Aler sans avoir saufconduis.
Adonc Amour et ses nourris
Auront de Dangier moins doubtance.
Et lors sentiray mon cueur rire,
Qui a present souvent souspire
En la prison de Desplaisance.

en pastis, literally, in inferior pasture.
saufconduis: anyone coming to Charles with supplies or letters or going to France to execute any commissions for him had to be granted special safe-conducts by the English government, and this naturally slowed up and rendered selective his dealings with the outside world, to an exasperating degree.

My heart has sent out to seek
All his well-wishers and friends;
He wishes to hold his great council
With their help, in order to have advice
How he may
Overcome and soon discomfit his enemies
Care, Mourning, and their allies,
Who wish to destroy him
In the prison of Discontent.

They have turned his delight into wasteland,
And put Joy on meagre rations
But Comfort, without fail, has
Again loyally promised him
That they will be conquered and banished;
From this Hope takes courage,
More than I dare tell;
This is what puts an end to his torment
In the prison of Discontent.

Soon may I see the time come,
I pray the God of Paradise,
That every man may go to his desire
Without having to have safe-conducts.
Then Love and those he has brought up in his household
Need have less fear of Dangier.
And then I shall feel my heart laughing,
Who now often sighs
In the prison of Discontent.

Pour ce que veoir ne vous puis,
Mon cueur se complaint jours et nuis,
Belle, nompareille de France,
Et m'a chargié de vous escrire
Qu'il n'a pas tout ce qu'il desire
En la prison de Desplaisance.

Since I may not see you,
My heart grieves day and night,
Fair peerless one of France,
And has charged me to write to you
Saying he has not all he desires
In the prison of Discontent.

Bvt late agoo went y my hert to se
As of his fare to haue sum knowlechyng
I fond him sett with hope in compane
That to him seide these wordis comfortyng
O hert be glad for y good tidyng brynge
So now let se pluk vp thi lustyhed
For whi y make the feithfulle trewe promys
That y thee kepe right sewrely out of drede
The hool tresoure of louys gret ricches

For this as trouthe to wite as do y thee
That the most fayrist borne or is lyvyng
She loueth thee of feithfulle fantase
And with good wille wolle doon to thi likyng
In alle to doon that is to hir sittyng
And these wordis sent thee of goodlihed
That spite of daungere or his gret rewdenes
She wol departe thee large maugre ther hed
The hool tresoure of louys gret ricches

For which my hert to say the trouthe parde
For ioy hath fett a thousand sithe sikyng
And thow to weren blak were vsid he
Yet was it then y-putt in forgetyng
And alle his woo his payne and turmentyng
In trust to fynde it now or he be ded
Bothe plesere comfort and gladnes
And only in his gouernaunce to lede
The hool tresoure of louys gret ricches

ricches, pronounce as French *richesse*.
sittyng, appropriate, suitable.
parde, a mild oath, though originally meaning 'By God'.
sithe, times.
fett . . . sikyng, heaved a sigh.
or, before.

My sabille hert with hope now blusshith reed
And for comfort of yow my fayre maystres
Which haue me promysid of yowre womanhed
The hool tresoure of louys gret ricches.

L'autr'ier alay mon cueur veoir,
Pour savoir comment se portoit;
Si trouvay avec lui Espoir
Qui doulcement le confortoit
Et ces parolles lui disoit:
'Cueur, tenez vous joieusement,
Je vous fais loyalle promesse
Que je vous garde seurement
Tresor d'amoureuse richesse.

'Car je vous fais pour vray savoir
Que la plus tresbelle qui soit
Vous ayme de loyal vouloir;
Et voulentiers pour vous feroit
Tout ce qu'elle faire pourroit;
Et vous mande que vrayement,
Maugré Dangier et sa rudesse,
Departir vous veult largement
Tresor d'amoureuse richesse.'

Alors mon cueur, pour dire voir,
De joye souvent soupiroit,
Et, combien qu'il portast le noir,
Toutesfoiz pour lors oublioit
Toute la doleur qu'il avoit,
Pensant de recouvrer briefment
Plaisance, Confort et Liesse,
Et d'avoir en gouvernement
Tresor [d'amoureuse richesse.]

A Bon Espoir mon cueur s'atent
Et a vous, ma belle maistresse,
Que lui espargniez loyaument
Tresor d'amoureuse richesse.

portast le noir, Charles had for many years made a point of always

The other day I went to see my heart,
To find out how he was;
I found Hope with him
Who was gently comforting him
And saying to him these words:
'Heart, behave joyfully,
I promise you loyally
That I am keeping for you safely
Treasure of love's riches.

'I tell you truly
That the fairest lady in the world
Loves you with loyal will;
And willingly would do for you
Anything she could;
And she sends to tell you that truly,
In spite of Dangier and his churlishness,
She wishes to give you a generous share of
The treasure of love's riches'.

Then my heart, to tell the truth,
Sighed many times for joy,
And although he was dressed in black,
Yet for that time forgot
All his pain,
Thinking that he would soon recover
Pleasance, Comfort and Delight,
And have and hold
The treasure of love's riches.

My heart waits on Good Hope
And on you, my fair mistress,
That you will fairly grant him
Treasure of love's riches.

appearing dressed in black at court functions, in mourning for his
unavenged father.

My poore hert bicomen is hermyte
In hermytage of thoughtfulle fantase
For false fortune so fulle of gret dispite
That many yere hath hatid him and me
Hath newe allyed hir this may y se
To his gret hurt with payne and heuynes
And hath him banysshid out of alle gladnes
That where to dwelle nath he o bidyng-place
Saue in the carfulle wode in payne to ly
Where he contentith bide his lyvis space
And yet y say him how it is foly

Moche haue y spent of speche to his profite
But that to harke y trowe he is not he
Mi wordis alle nar worthi to him a myte
His wille is sett in suche perplexitie
That lightly loo hit kan not chaungid be
So is he gouernyd al as bi distres
Which ganyst his profit doth neuyr cesse
Him to avise such counselle ist he hase
That nyght and day him holdith company
That he may not eschewe his wrecchid case
And yet y say him how it is foly

This as for me y cast to leue him quyt
Mi bestbilouyd myn hertis sovl lade

line 2. 'En l'ermitage de Pensee'.
payne and heuynes, Tristesse.
line 9. 'Fors ou boys de Merencolie'; in the English MS *wode* is a correction from *end*.
line 13. 'Mais il ne l'a point escoutee'.
nar, are not.
line 21. 'De si pres lui tient compaignie (Destresse)/Qu'il ne peut ennuy delaissier'.
line 23. 'Pour ce, sachiez, je m'en acquitte'.
sovl, only.

Without so be ye lust to him write
Sum praty word of yowre benygne bounte
Forto alesse his gret aduersite
Ellis hath he made a feithfulle trewe promys
Forto renounce the ioy and gret ricches
Of gladsom thought or plesere in him was
And aftir that vnto that howre he dey
The abite of discomfort on him lace
And yet y say him how it is foly

O fayre sance per lo this without yowre grace
For any thyng that y kan do trewly
My dullid hert wol not comfort allas
And yet y say him how it is foly

line 27. 'Dont sa doleur soit allegee'.
line 30. 'De Plaisir et de Doulx Penser'.
line 31f. 'Et aprés ce, toute sa vie,/L'abit de Desconfort porter'.
sance per, unparalleled, without equal.

Par le commandment d'Amours
Et de la plus belle de France,
J'enforcis mon chastel tousjours
Appellé Joyeuse Plaisance,
Assis sur roche d'Esperance;
Avitaillié l'ay de Confort;
Contre Dangier et sa puissance
Je le tendray jusqu'a la mort.

En ce chastel y a trois tours,
Dont l'une se nomme Fiance
D'avoir briefment loyal secours,
Et la seconde Souvenance,
La tierce Ferme Desirance.
Ainsi le chastel est si fort
Que nul n'y peut faire grevance;
Je le tendray jusqu'a la mort.

Combien que Dangier, par faulx tours,
De le m'oster souvent s'avance,
Mais il trouvera le rebours,
Se Dieu plaist, de sa mal vueillance.
Bon Droit est de mon aliance,
Loyauté et lui sont d'accort
De m'aidier; pour ce, sans doubtance
Je le tendray jusqu'a la mort.

Faisons bon guet sans decevance
Et assaillons par ordonnance,
Mon cueur, Dangier qui nous fait tort;
Se prandre le puis par vaillance,
Je le tendray jusqu'a la mort!

At the command of Love
And of the fairest lady in France
I am strengthening my castle
Named Joyous Pleasance
Founded on the rock of Hope;
I have stocked it with Comfort;
Against Dangier and his power
I shall hold it till I die.

In this castle are three towers,
One called Trust
That I shall soon have loyal help,
And the second Memory,
And the third Constant Longing.
Thus the castle is so strong
That no-one can harm it;
I shall hold it till I die.

Although Dangier by deceitful tricks
Often approaches to take it from me,
He will find the reward,
If it so please God, of his ill intentions.
Good Right is on my side,
Loyalty and he have agreed
To help me; wherefore, without doubt,
I shall hold it till I die.

Let us keep good watch without deceit
And attack in due form,
My heart, Dangier that wrongs us;
If I can capture him by valiance,
I shall hold him till I die

(*or*, until he dies).

Allas allas how is hit heth gen entresse
Vnto myn hert this woful tidyngis here
For told him is to his gret heuynes
That his most fayre and goodly swete hert dere
Whom he hath long tyme servid feithfully
O welaway doth now in seeknes ly
For which dispeyre he doth him silf confound
Wisshing that he were depe graue vndir ground
And saith how that his lijf doth him ennoy.

I oft haue goon to comfort him dowtles
And bad him take no drede nor displesere
For what bi goddis grace to his gladnes
That hit nys deedly seeknes shalle he here
And that she shalle be helid hastily
But what y say he settith not therby
Saue wayle and wepe and prayeth in euery stounde
That he were in his wyndyng-shete y-wounde
And saith how that his lijf doth him ennoy.

When y say him he shulde leue his distres
For fortune nys so crewelle of manere
To robbe this world of so gret a ricches
Which is yowre verry lod-sterre here & stere
Of eche good thyng that hath more then plenty
But what he saith to trust is gret foly
On fortune which doth turne hir whele so round
This is comfort that y haue in him found
And saith how that is lijf doth him ennoy.

God of thi grace o thou god most myghti
Harkith myn hert which prayeth thee humbly

how is hit heth gen entresse, who is it has given entrance to.
graue, buried.
stere, guide, S.

48

To suffir deth geue him his fatalle wound
Thus is he greid/woo doth him so abound
And saith how that his lijf doth him ennoy.

greid, determined, resolved.

Helas! helas! qui a laissié entrer
Devers mon cueur Doloreuse Nouvelle?
Conté lui a plainement, sans celer,
Que sa Dame, la tresplaisant et belle,
Qu'il a long temps tresloyaument servie,
Est a present en griefve maladie;
Dont il est cheu en desespoir si fort
Qu'il souhaide piteusement la mort
Et dit qu'il est ennuyé de sa vie.

Je suis alé pour le reconforter,
En lui priant qu'il n'ait nul soussy d'elle,
Car, se Dieu plaist, il orra brief conter
Que ce n'est pas maladie mortelle,
Et que sera prochainement guerye.
Mais ne lui chault de chose que lui dye,
Ainçois en pleurs a tousjours son ressort
Par Tristesse, qui asprement le mort,
Et dit qu'il est ennuyé de sa vie.

Quant je lui dy qu'il ne se doit doubter,
Car Fortune n'est pas si trescruelle,
Qu'elle voulsist hors de ce monde oster
Celle qui est des princesses l'estoille,
Qui partout luist des biens dont est garnie,
Il me respond qu'il est foul qui se fie
En Fortune, qui a fait maint tort.
Ainsi ne voult recevoir reconfort
Et dit qu'il est ennuyé de sa vie.

Dieu tout puissant, par vostre courtoisie,
Guerissez la, ou mon cueur vous supplie
Que vous souffrez que la mort son effort
Face sur lui, car il en est d'accord
Et dit qu'il est ennuyé de sa vie.

Alas, alas, who has let in
Sorrowful News to visit my heart?
He has told him plainly, without hiding anything,
That his Lady, the charming and fair,
Whom he has long served most loyally,
Is now in grievous sickness;
At this he is fallen into such despair
That pitifully he asks for death
And says he is aweary of his life.

I went to comfort him,
Begging him to have no anxiety about her,
For, if God pleases, he will soon hear
That it is no deadly sickness,
And that she will be soon cured.
But he cares nothing for what I say to him,
But turns again to weeping
Because of Sadness, that stings him cruelly,
And says he is aweary of his life.

When I tell him that he must not fear,
For Fortune is not so over-cruel
As to wish to take from this world
That star of princesses,
That shines everywhere by the virtues that adorn her,
He replies that a man is mad who trusts
In Fortune, who has wronged many a one.
Thus he will receive no consolation
And says he is aweary of his life.

Almighty God, by your courtesy,
Cure her, or my heart begs you
To allow death to do his worst to him
For he agrees to this
And says he is aweary of his life.

In Ballade LVI the lady is better, and the refrain is *'Saint Gabriel, bonne nouvelle!'*, but in LVII she is dead, and the envoy prays:

> Dieu, sur tout souverain Seigneur,
> Ordonnez, par grace et doulceur,
> De l'ame d'elle, tellement,
> Qu'elle ne soit pas longuement
> En paine, soussy, et doleur!

Steele p. 69; no French equivalent

In slepe ben leyd alle song daunce or disport
Also prays of bewte bote or gantilesse
Now deth allas hath to my discomfort
Enrayfid me my lady and maystres
A woofull hert whos sorow kan not cesse
Round with hir deth thou shulde haue tan thi bere
Dwellyng no more with ioy nor yet gladnes
For without hir of nought now lyue y here

O myghti god what am y quyk or deed
Nay certis deed this am y verry sewre
For fele y plesere ioy nor lustihed
Wo worthe the fate of my mysaventure
Nought lak y now but clothe my sepulture
O clothe me care-sewte of my ladi dere
That fynde my silf an outcast creature
For without hir of nought now lyue y here

Me thynkith right as a syphir now y serue
That nombre makith and is him silf noon

bote, profit, advantage, S.
Enrayfid, stolen.
A is exclamatory in line 5.
Round with, together with, S.
care-sewte, mourning clothes.

O cursid deth whi nelt thou do me sterue
Syn my swet hert/syn my good sowl is goon
Now may y say alone y goo alon
Savyng with sorow payne and displesere
With whos deth/all welthe bicame my foon
For without hir of nought now lyue y here

I kepe no more of lijf then were my right
Forwhi hit were extorcioun in manere
Wherfore y wolde my lijf sum nedy wight
Hit had/for now of nought as lyue y here

nelt thou do me sterue, will you not make me die.
welthe, happiness, S.

This is followed by 'Alone am y and wille to be alone', which is
perhaps imitated from a ballad by Christine de Pisan, and 'For dedy
lijf my lyvy deth y wite', which has no French original that we know.

Ofte in my thought fulle besily haue y sought
Ayens the bigynnyng of this fresshe newe yere
What praty thyng that y best yeven ought
To hir that was myn hertis lady dere
But alle that thought bitane is fro me clere
Sith deth allas hath closid hir vndir cley
And hath this world fornakid with hir here
God haue hir sowle y kan no bettir say

But forto kepe in custome lo my thought
And of my sely seruice the manere
In shewyng allys that y forget hir nought
Vnto eche wight y shall to my powere
This dede hir serue with massis and prayere
For a to fowle a shame were me mafay
Hir to forgete this tyme that neigheth nere
God haue hir sowle y kan no bettir say

To hir profit now nys ther to ben bought
Noon othir thyng alle wol y bay hit dere
Wherefore thou lord that lordist alle aloft
Mi deedis take suche as goodnes stere
And crowne hir lord within thyn hevenly spere
As for most trewist lady may y say
Most good most fayre and most benygne of chere
God haue hir sowle y kan no bettir say

When y hir prayse/or praysyng of hir here
Alle though it whilom were to me plesere
Hit fille y-nough hit doth myn hert to-day

yeven, to give.
here (line 7), may be an unrecorded coinage meaning 'stealing away, rape, theft', or an error for *bere*, S.
mafay, by my faith.
alle wol y bay, although I am willing to buy.

And doth me wisshe y clothid had my bere
God haue hir sowle y kan no bettir say

clothid, made ready, S.

This is a somewhat expanded translation of the French poem, the
main difference being that the envoi of the latter says simply:

> Quant je pense a la renommee
> Des grans biens dont estoit paree,
> Mon povre cueur de dueil se pasme;
> De lui souvent est regrettee;
> Je pry a Dieu qu'il en ait l'ame.

paree, adorned.
se pasme, swoons.

When y revolue in my remembraunce
The bewte shappe and the swete eyen tayne
Of hir y callid myn hert hool plesaunce
My lyvis ioy my sovl lady souerayne
Of eche good thewe that was the fressh fountayne
Which newly deth hath tane o welaway
For which y say with wepyng eyen tay
That this world nys but even a thyng in vayne

In tyme a-past ther ran gret renomaunce
Of dido cresseid Alcest and Eleyne
And many moo as fynde we in romaunce
That were of bewte huge and welbesayne
But in the ende allas to thynke agayne
How deth hem slew and sleth moo day bi day
Hit doth me wel aduert this may y say
That this world nys but even a thyng in vayne

Me thenkith that deth cast bi his gouernaunce
Forto distroy alle worldly plesere playne
Forwhi he doth therto his gret puysshaunce
That hath allas so moche fayre folkis slayne
And dayly slethe/what ioy doth he refrayne
Out of this world and bryngith in such dismay
For without them y iuge this mafay
That this world nys but even a thyng in vayne

tayne, *tay*, two.
hert, heart's.
sovl, only.
thewe, quality.
playne, completely.
refrayne, remove, or withhold, S.
mafay, by my faith.

O god of loue thou may perseyue certayne
To myn entent that deth thee warrith ay
So se y wel but though hit menden may
That this world nys but even a thyng in vayne

but though, (that) unless.

Quant Souvenir me ramentoit
La grant beauté dont estoit plaine,
Celle que mon cueur appelloit
Sa seule Dame souveraine,
De tous biens la vraye fontaine,
Qui est morte nouvellement,
Je dy, en pleurant tendrement,
Ce monde n'est que chose vaine!

Ou vieil temps grant renom couroit
De Creseide, Yseud, Elaine
Et maintes autres qu'on nommoit
Parfaittes en beauté haultaine.
Mais, au derrain, en son demaine
La Mort les prist piteusement;
Par quoy puis veoir clerement
Ce monde n'est que chose vaine.

La Mort a voulu et vouldroit,
Bien le congnois, mettre sa paine
De destruire, s'elle povoit,
Liesse et Plaisance Mondaine,
Quant tant de belles dames maine
Hors du monde; car vrayement
Sans elles, a mon jugement,
Ce monde n'est que chose vaine.

Amours, pour verité certaine,
Mort vous guerrie fellement;
Se n'y trouvez amendement,
Ce monde n'est que chose vaine.

When Memory recalled to me
The great beauty that filled
Her whom my heart used to call
His only sovereign Lady,
True fountain of all goodness,
Who died not long ago,
I said, weeping tenderly,
This world is nothing but a vain thing.

In the old time great fame was noised abroad
Of Cressid, Yseult, Elaine, (or Helen)
And many other ladies that were called
Perfect in lofty beauty.
But at the last into her realm
Death took them, unhappily;
Wherefore I can clearly see
This world is nothing but a vain thing.

Death has wished and still would wish,
I know well, to expend all her efforts
In destroying, if she could,
Delight and Worldly Pleasure,
When she leads so many lovely ladies
Out of the world; for truly,
Without them, it seems to me,
This world is nothing but a vain thing.

Love, it is a certain truth,
Death makes bitter, cruel war on you;
If you can put no end to this,
This world is nothing but a vain thing.

It almost seems *de rigueur* to compare this with Villon's '*Ballade des Dames du Temps Jadis*', although it was written several decades earlier and more manifestly draws some of its inspiration from a personal bereavement; it may more profitably be compared with other, earlier poems that elaborate the *Ubi sunt* theme, such as: 'Hwer is paris & heleyne/that weren so bryht & feyre on bleo,/ Amadas & dideyne,/tristram, yseude and alle theo/. . . heo beoth i-glyden vt of the reyne . . .' It is in a much lighter, more courtly and less erudite tone than Villon's piece, in which the witty complimentary *pointe* at the end of verse 3 would seem shockingly out of place.

Steele p. 78, Champion p. 95. Compare with the French text.

> I haue the obit of my lady dere
> Made in the chirche of loue fulle solempnely
> And for hir sowle the service and prayere
> In thought waylyng haue songe hit hevyly
> The torchis sett of sighis pitously
> Which was with sorow sett a-flame
> The tovmbe is made als to the same
> Of karfulle cry depayntid alle with teeris
> The which richely is write about
> That here lo lith withouten dowt
> The hool tresoure of alle wordly blys

> Of gold on hir ther lith an ymage clere
> With safyr blew y-sett so inrichely
> For hit is write and seide how the safere
> Doth token trouthe and gold to ben happy
> The which that wel bisettith hir hardily
> Forwhi hit was an ewrous trewe madame
> And of goodnes ay flowren may hir name
> For god the which that made hir lo y-wys

bisettith, is appropritate to.
ewrous, fortunate, S.

To make such oon my thynke a myght ben prowt
For lo she was/as right well be she mowt.
The hool tresoure of alle wordly blys

O pese no more myn hert astoneth here
To here me prayse hir vertu so trewly
Of hir that had no fawt withouten were
As alle the world hit saith as welle as y
The which that knew hir deedis inthorowly
God hath hir tane y trowe for hir good fame
His hevene the more to ioy with sport and game
The more to plese and comfort his seyntis
For certis welle may she comfort a rowt
Noou is she saynt she was here so devowt
The hool tresoure of alle worldly blys

Not vaylith now though y complayne this
Al most we deye therto so lete vs lowt
For ay to kepe ther is no wight so stowt
The hool tresoure of alle worldly blys

withouten were, without doubt.
Al most we deye (MS. *Almost*), we must all die.

The sapphire generally stands for hope; it delivers prisoners if used
correctly, and must be worn very chastely. 'He hathe vertu to
confort & glade the hert therfor' and helps against melancholy
passions, evil humours, and poison. 'Also this ston dothe away
sorow and dred . . . and it maketh the hert stedfast in godnes, &
it maketh a man meke & myld & godly' (*Peterborough Lapidary*).

J'ay fait l'obseque de ma Dame
Dedens le moustier amoureux,
Et le service pour son ame
A chanté Penser Doloreux;
Mains sierges de Soupirs Piteux
Ont esté en son luminaire;
Aussi j'ay fait la tombe faire
De Regrez, tous de lermes pains;
Et tout entour, moult richement,
Est escript, Cy gist vrayement
Le tresor de tous biens mondains.

Dessus elle gist une lame
Faicte d'or et de saffirs bleux,
Car saffir est nommé la jame
De Loyauté, et l'or eureux.
Bien lui appartiennent ces deux,
Car Eur et Loyauté pourtraire
Voulu, en la tresdebonnaire,
Dieu qui la fist de ses deux mains,
Et fourma merveilleusement;
C'estoit, a parler plainnement,
Le tresor de tous biens mondains.

N'en parlons plus; mon cueur se pasme
Quant il oyt les fais vertueux
D'elle, qui estoit sans nul blasme,
Comme jurent celles et ceulx
Qui congnoissoyent ses conseulx;
Si croy que Dieu la voulu traire
Vers lui, pour parer son repaire
De Paradis ou sont les saints;
Car c'est d'elle bel parement,
Que l'en nommoit communement
Le tresor de tous biens mondains.

I have held the funeral service of my Lady
In the minster of Love,
And the service for her soul
Was sung by Grieving Thought;
Many candles of Pitiful Sighs
Were in the offering of lights;
And I had the tomb made
Of Regrets all painted with tears;
And all around right richly
Is inscribed, Here lies truly
The treasure of all worldly good.

Above her lies a slab
Made of gold and blue sapphires,
For sapphire is named the gem
Of Loyalty, and gold fortunate.
To her rightly these two belong,
For to portray Good Fortune and Loyalty
In this most noble lady, was the wish of
God who made her with His two hands,
And fashioned wondrously;
She was, to speak it plainly,
The treasure of all worldly good.

Let us speak no more of her; my heart swoons
When he hears (of) the virtuous deeds
Of her that was without blame,
As they swear, men and women,
That knew her counsels;
Thus I believe that God wished to draw her
Towards Himself, to ornament his dwelling
Of Paradise where the saints are;
For she would be a fine decoration,
Whom everyone used to call
The treasure of all worldly good.

De riens ne servent plours ne plains;
Tous mourrons, ou tart ou briefment;
Nul ne peut garder longuement
Le tresor de tous biens mondains.

Weeping nor mourning serve any purpose;
We shall all die, late or soon;
No man can keep for long
The treasure of all worldly good.

In the forest of noyous hevynes
As y went wandryng in the moneth of may
I mette of loue the myghti gret goddes
Which axid me whithir y was away
I hir answerid as fortune doth convey
As oon exilid from ioy al be me loth
That passyng welle alle folke me clepyn may
The man forlost that wot not where he goth

Half in a smyle ayen of hir humblesse
She seide my frend if so y wist ma fay
Wherfore that thou art brought in such distresse
To shape thyn ese y wolde my silf assay
For here-tofore y sett thyn hert in way
Of gret plesere y not whoo made thee wroth
Hit grevith me/thee see in suche aray
The man forlost that wot not where he goth

Allas y seide most souereyne good princesse
Ye knowe my case what nedith to yow say
Hit is thorugh deth that shewith to alle rudesse
Hath fro me tane that y most louyd ay
In whom that alle myn hope and comfort lay
So passyng frendship was bitwene vs both
That y was not/to fals deth did hir day
The man forlost that wot not where he goth

Thus am y blynd allas and welaway
Al fer myswent with my staf grapsyng wey

For the setting, cf. Virgil, *Aeneid* I, 305ff.
ma fay, by my faith.
y not, I do not know.
to fals deth did hir day, until false Death made her die.
fer myswent, far gone astray; S. says 'for fear of going astray'.
grapsyng wey, groping, feeling the way.

66

That no thyng axe but me a graue to cloth
For pite is that y lyue thus a day
The man forlost that wot not where he goth

En la forest d'Ennuyeuse Tristesse,
Un jour m'avint qu'a part moy cheminoye,
Si rencontray l'Amoureuse Deesse
Qui m'appella, demandant ou j'aloye.
Je respondy que, par Fortune, estoye
Mis en exil en ce bois, long temps a,
Et qu'a bon droit appeller me povoye
L'omme esgaré qui ne scet ou il va.

En sousriant, par sa tresgrant humblesse,
Me respondy, 'Amy, se je savoye
Pourquoy tu es mis en ceste destresse,
A mon povair voulentiers t'ayderoye;
Car, ja pieça, je mis ton cueur en voye
De tout plaisir, ne sçay qui l'en osta;
Or me desplaist qu'a present je te voye
L'omme esgaré qui ne scet ou il va.'

'Helas!' dis je, 'souverainne Princesse,
Mon fait savés, pourquoy le vous diroye?
C'est par la Mort qui fait a tous rudesse,
Qui m'a tollu celle que tant amoye,
En qui estoit tout l'espoir que j'avoye,
Qui me guidoit, si bien m'acompaigna
En son vivant, que point ne me trouvoye
L'omme esgaré qui ne scet ou il va.

'Aveugle suy, ne sçay ou aler doye;
De mon baston, affin que ne forvoye,
Je vois tastant mon chemin ça et la;
C'est grant pitié qu'il couvient que je soye
L'omme esgaré qui ne scet ou il va.'

In the forest of Wearisome Sadness
I happened one day to be journeying alone,
And met the Goddess of Love,
Who called to me, asking where I was going.
I replied that because of Fortune I had been
Long since exiled in this wood,
And that I could rightly call myself
The lost man that knows not where he is going.

Smiling, in her graciousness
She replied to me, 'My friend, if I knew
Why you are in this distress,
Willingly I should help you as much as I could;
For not long ago I set your heart on the road
Towards all pleasure, I know not who took him thence;
It displeases me that now I see (in) you
The lost man that knows not where he is going.'

'Alas!' said I, 'sovereign Princess,
You know my case, why should I tell it to you?
It is through Death that does violence to all,
Who has taken from me her I loved so much,
In whom was all the hope I had,
Who guided me and accompanied me so well
When she was alive, that I was not
The lost man that knows not where he is going.

'I am blind, and know not where I should go;
With my stick, lest I wander from the path,
I go tapping out my way here and there;
It is great pity that I must be
The lost man that knows not where he is going.'

Whan fresshe phebus day of seynt valentyne
Had whirlid vp his golden chare aloft
The burnyd bemys of it gan to shyne
In at my chambre where y slepid soft
Of which the light that he had with him brought
He wook me of the slepe of heuynes
Wherin forslepid y alle the nyght dowtles
Vpon my bed so hard of newous thought

Of which this day to parten there bottyne
An oost of fowlis semblid in a croft
Myn neye biside and pletid ther latyne
To haue with them as nature had them wrought
Ther makis forto wrappe in wyngis soft
For which they gan so loude ther cries dresse
That y ne koude not slepe in my distres
Vpon my bed so hard of newous thought

Tho gan y reyne with teeris of myn eyne
Mi pilowe and to wayle and cursen oft
My destyny and gan my look enclyne
These birdis to/and seide ye birdis ought

The French begins, 'Le beau souleil, le jour saint Valentin/Qui apportoit sa chandelle alumee'.
burnyd, burnished.
Of which the light—S. suggests this means 'by which light', and that 'of which' is just used as a vague connective. The refrain in the French is 'Sur le dur lit d'Ennuïeuse Pensee'.
bottyne, spoils, gains.
neye, eye.
pletid, pleaded in.
makis, mates.
In the French, he says to the birds, 'Oyseaulx, je vous voy en chemin/De tout plaisir et joye desiree;/Chascun de vous a per qui

To thanke nature where as it sittith me nought
That han yowre makis to yowre gret gladnes
Where y sorow the deth of my maystres
Vpon my bed so hard of newous thought

Als wele is him this day that hath him kaught
A valentyne that louyth him as y gesse
Where as this comfort sole y here me dresse
Vpon my bed so hard of newous thought

lui agree,/Et point n'en ay, car Mort, qui m'a trahy,/A prins mon
per, dont en dueil je languy . . .'
it sittith me nought, it is not suitable for me.

Balades, chançons et complaintes
Sont pour moy mises en oubly,
Car ennuy et pensees maintes
M'ont tenu long temps endormy.
Non pour tant, pour passer soussy,
Essaier vueil se je sauroye
Rimer, ainsi que je souloye.
Au meins j'en feray mon povoir,
Combien que je congnois et sçay
Que mon langage trouveray
Tout enroillié de Nonchaloir.

Plaisans parolles sont estaintes
En moy qui deviens rassoty;
Au fort, je vendray aux attaintes
Quant beau parler m'aura failly;
Pour quoy pry ceulx qui m'ont oy
Langagier, quant pieça j'estoy
Jeune, novel et plain de joye,
Que vueillent excusé m'avoir.
Oncques mais je ne me trouvay
Si rude, car je suis, pour vray,
Tout enroillié de Nonchaloir.

Amoureux ont parolles paintes
Et langage frois et joly;
Plaisance dont ilz sont accointes
Parle pour eux; en ce party
J'ay esté, or n'est plus ainsi;
Alors de beau parler trouvoye
A bon marchié tant que vouloye;
Si ay despendu mon savoir,
Et s'un peu espargnié en ay,
Il est, quant vendra a l'essay,
Tout enroillié de Nonchaloir.

Ballads, songs and laments
Are put away and forgotten for me,
For weariness and many thoughts
Have held me long asleep.
And yet, to pass the unhappy time,
I should like to try whether I am able to
Rhyme as I used to.
At least I shall do what I can,
Although I know and recognise
That I shall find my language
All rusted over with Nonchaloir.

Pleasant words are extinguished
In me, who am becoming dull;
Yet I shall achieve my ends
When fair talk has deserted me.
Wherefore I pray those who have heard me
An elegant talker, when long ago I was
Young, new and full of joy,
To be kind enough to excuse me.
Never before did I find myself
So rough, for I am truly
All rusted over with Nonchaloir.

Those in love have painted words
And fresh, pretty language;
Pleasure with whom they are familiar
Speaks for them; I used to be
One of their number, but now no more;
Then I could find sweet talk
Cheaply, as much as I wanted;
Thus I have spent my wit,
And if I have saved a little
It proves, when it comes to the test,
All rusted over with Nonchaloir.

Mon jubilé faire devoye,
Mais on diroit que me rendroye
Sans coup ferir, car Bon Espoir
M'a dit que renouvelleray;
Pour ce, mon cueur fourbir feray
Tout enroillié de Nonchaloir.

I ought to celebrate my jubilee
(my fifty years, my retirement from love)
But people would say I was surrendering
Without striking a blow, since Good Hope
Has told me that I shall grow new again;
So I shall have my heart cleaned and polished,
(that is) All rusted over with Nonchaloir.

En regardant vers le païs de France,
Un jour m'avint, a Dovre sur la mer,
Qu'il me souvint de la doulce plaisance
Que souloye oudit pays trouver;
Si commençay de cueur a souspirer,
Combien certes que grant bien me faisoit
De voir France que mon cueur amer doit.

Je m'avisay que c'estoit non savance
De telz souspirs dedens mon cueur garder,
Veu que je voy que la voye commence
De bonne paix, qui tous biens peut donner;
Pour ce, tournay en confort mon penser.
Mais non pourtant mon cueur ne se lassoit
De voir France que mon cueur amer doit.

Alors chargay en la nef d'Esperance
Tous mes souhaitz, en leur priant d'aler
Oultre la mer, sans faire demourance,
Et a France de me recommander.
Or nous doint Dieu bonne paix sans tarder!
Adonce auray loisir, mais qu'ainsi soit,
De voir France que mon cueur amer doit.

Paix est tresor qu'on ne peut trop loer;
Je hé guerre, point ne la doy prisier;
Destourbé m'a long temps, soit tort ou droit,
De voir France que mon cueur amer doit.

Looking towards the land of France,
One day it happened, at Dover on the sea,
That I remembered the sweet delight
That I used to find in that land;
So I began to sigh from my heart,
Although it certainly did me great good
To see France that my heart must love.

I realised that it was foolishness
To keep such sighs within my heart,
When I see the way begun
Of good peace, that may give us all good.
For this, I turned my thought to comfort,
But nevertheless my heart did not weary
Of seeing France that my heart must love.

Then I loaded into the ship of Hope
All my wishes, praying them to go
Beyond the sea, making no delay,
And to remember me to France.
Now may God give us good peace without waiting!
Then I shall have leisure, may it be so,
To see France that my heart must love.

Peace is a treasure one cannot praise too much;
I hate war, and should esteem it nothing at all;
It has hindered me a long time, rightly or wrongly,
From seeing France that my heart must love.

Priés pour paix, doulce Vierge Marie,
Royne des cieulx, et du monde maistresse,
Faictes prier, par vostre courtoisie,
Saints et saintes, et prenés vostre adresse
Vers vostre filz, requerant sa haultesse
Qu'il lui plaise son peuple regarder,
Que de son sang a voulu racheter,
En deboutant guerre qui tout desvoye;
De prieres ne vous vueilliez lasser;
Priez pour paix, le vray tresor de joye!

Priez, prelas et gens de sainte vie,
Religieux ne dormez en peresse,
Priez, maistres et tous suivans clergie,
Car par guerre fault que l'estude cesse;
Moustiers destruis sont sans qu'on les redresse,
Le service de Dieu vous fault laissier.
Quant ne povez en repos demourer,
Priez si fort que briefment Dieu vous oye;
L'Eglise voult a ce vous ordonner.
Priez pour paix, le vray tresor de joye!

Priez, princes qui avez seigneurie,
Roys, ducs, contes, barons plains de noblesse,
Gentilz hommes avec chevalerie,
Car meschans gens surmontent gentillesse;
En leurs mains ont toute vostre richesse,
Debatz les font en hault estat monter,
Vous le povez chascun jour veoir au cler,
Et sont riches de voz biens et monnoye
Dont vous deussiez le peuple suporter.
Priez pour paix, le vray tresor de joye!

Priez, peuple qui souffrez tirannie,
Car voz seigneurs sont en telle foiblesse
Qu'ilz ne peuent vous garder, par maistrie,

78

Pray for peace, sweet Virgin Mary,
Queen of heaven and mistress of this world,
Of your courtesy cause to pray
All the saints, and make your prayer
To your son, requesting his highness
To be pleased to look upon his people,
That he willingly redeemed with his blood,
And drive out war that throws everything out of true;
Weary not of prayers,
Pray for peace, the true treasure of joy!

Pray, prelates and folk of holy life,
Monks, sleep not in sloth,
Pray, masters and all clerks that follow learning,
For war brings studies to an end;
Minsters are destroyed and no-one restores them,
You are forced to desert God's service.
When you cannot rest in quiet,
Pray so hard that God may quickly hear you;
The Church sets you this task.
Pray for peace, the true treasure of joy!

Pray, princes that bear rule,
Kings, dukes, earls, barons full of nobleness,
High-born men of chivalry,
For wicked men are overcoming nobility;
They hold all your riches in their hands,
Lawsuits raise them high in rank,
You may see this clearly every day,
And they are rich in your goods and incomes
With which you should be supporting the common people.
Pray for peace, the true treasure of joy!

Pray, people that suffer tyranny,
For your lords have become so weak
That they cannot protect you by their mastery

Ne vous aidier en vostre grant destresse;
Loyaulx marchans, la selle si vous blesse
Fort sur le dox; chascun vous vient presser
Et ne povez marchandise mener,
Car vous n'avez seur passage ne voye,
Et maint peril vous couvient il passer.
Priez pour paix, le vray tresor de joye!

Priez, galans joyeux en compaignie,
Qui despendre desirez a largesse;
Guerre vous tient la bourse desgarnie.
Priez, amans, qui voulez en liesse
Servir amours, car guerre, par rudesse,
Vous destourbe de voz dames hanter,
Qui maintesfoiz fait leurs vouloirs tourner;
Et quant tenez le bout de la couroye,
Un estrangier si le vous vient oster;
Priez pour paix, le vray tresor de joye!

Dieu tout puissant nous vueille conforter
Toutes choses en terre, ciel et mer;
Priez vers lui que brief en tout pourvoye,
En lui seul est de tous maulx amender;
Priez pour paix, le vray tresor de joye!

Nor help you in your great distress.
Honest merchants, the saddle presses painfully
On your backs; everyone oppresses you
And you cannot move your goods about
For there is no way or road safe,
And you are forced to brave many dangers.
Pray for peace, the true treasure of joy!

Pray, gallants that enjoy good company,
Who long to spend money freely;
War keeps your purses ill-supplied.
Pray, lovers who wish to serve Love
In happiness, for war by its harshness
Hinders you from attending on your ladies,
Which often makes them change their minds;
And when you have got hold of the end of the cord
A stranger comes and takes it out of your hand.
Pray for peace, the true treasure of joy!

May almighty God comfort us
And all things in heaven, earth, or sea;
Pray Him that He may soon provide for all,
In Him alone is the power to amend all ills;
Pray for peace, the true treasure of joy!

Je fu en fleur ou temps passé d'enfance,
Et puis aprés devins fruit en jeunesse;
Lors m'abaty de l'arbre de Plaisance,
Vert et non meur, Folie, ma maistresse.
Et pour cela, Raison qui tout redresse
A son plaisir, sans tort ou mesprison,
M'a a bon droit, par sa tresgrant sagesse,
Mis pour meurir ou feurre de prison.

En ce j'ay fait longue continuance,
Sans estre mis a l'essor de Largesse;
J'en suy contant et tiens que, sans doubtance,
C'est pour le mieulx, combien que par peresse
Deviens fletry et tire vers vieillesse.
Assez estaint est en moy le tison
De sot desir, puis qu'ay esté en presse
Mis pour meurir ou feurre de prison.

Dieu nous doint paix, car c'est ma desirance!
Adonc seray en l'eaue de Liesse
Tost refreschi, et au souleil de France
Bien nettié du moisy de Tristesse;
J'attens Bon Temps, endurant en humblesse.
Car j'ay espoir que Dieu ma guerison
Ordonnera; pour ce, m'a sa haultesse
Mis pour meurir ou feurre de prison.

Fruit suis d'yver qui a meins de tendresse
Que fruit d'esté; si suis en garnison,
Pour amolir ma trop verde duresse,
Mis pour meurir ou feurre de prison.

I was in flower in the past time of childhood,
And after became a fruit in my youth;
Then Folly my mistress beat me down from the tree
Of Pleasance while I was still green and not ripe.
And for this, Reason who redresses all
At her pleasure without wrong or misprision,
Quite rightly in her great wisdom
Set me to ripen in the straw of prison.

Here I have long remained
Without being allowed to soar off into Freedom;
I am content and consider it is doubtless
For the best, although through sloth (idleness, disuse)
I am becoming wrinkled and drawing towards old age.
Extinguished in me pretty well is the torch
Of foolish desire, since I have been put in store
Set to ripen in the straw of prison.

God give us peace, for that is my desire!
Then I shall be in the waters of Delight
Quickly refreshed, and in the sunlight of France
Well cleaned of the mould of Sadness;
I await Good Time, enduring in humbleness,
For I have hope that God will ordain
My cure; for this, his majesty
Set me to ripen in the straw of prison.

I am a winter fruit that has less tenderness
Than summer fruit, so I am kept in store
To soften my too green hardness,
Set to ripen in the straw of prison.

winter fruit—born in late November.

Nouvelles ont couru en France
Par mains lieux que j'estoye mort;
Dont avoient peu desplaisance
Aucuns qui me hayent a tort;
Autres en ont eu desconfort,
Qui m'ayment de loyal vouloir,
Comme mes bons et vrais amis.
Si fais a toutes gens savoir
Qu'encore est vive la souris!

Je n'ay eu ne mal ne grevance,
Dieu mercy, mais suis sain et fort,
Et passe temps en esperance
Que paix, qui trop longuement dort,
S'esveillera, et par accort
A tous fera liesse avoir.
Pour ce, de Dieu soient maudis
Ceulx qui sont dolens de veoir
Qu'encore est vive la souris!

Jeunesse sur moy a puissance,
Mais Vieillesse fait son effort
De m'avoir en sa gouvernance;
A present faillira son sort.
Je suis assez loing de son port,
De pleurer vueil garder mon hoir;
Loué soit Dieu de Paradis,
Qui m'a donné force et povoir
Qu'encore est vive la souris!

Nul ne porte pour moy le noir,
On vent meillieur marchié drap gris;
Or tiengne chascun, pour tout voir,
Qu'encore est vive la souris!

News has gone about in France
In many places, that I was dead;
Which gave little displeasure to some,
Some who hate me wrongfully;
Others were quite distressed by it,
Who loyally love me
As good true friends.
So I am letting everybody know
That the mouse is still alive!

I have had neither ill nor pain,
Thank God, but am well and strong,
And spend my time hoping
That peace, who sleeps too long,
Will awake, and by agreement
Make everyone joyful.
So may they be cursed by God
Who are grieved to see
That the mouse is still alive!

Youth has power over me,
But Old Age is making the effort
To get me under her rule;
Now her attempt will fail.
I am far enough from her harbour,
And wish to keep my heir from weeping;
Praised be God of Paradise
Who has given me strength and power,
That the mouse is still alive!

Let no-one wear black for me,
They sell grey more cheaply;
Let everyone consider it quite true
That the mouse is still alive!

En tirant d'Orleans a Blois,
L'autre jour par eaue venoye.
Si rencontré, par plusieurs foiz,
Vaisseaux, ainsi que je passoye,
Qui singloient leur droicte voye
Et aloient legierement,
Pour ce qu'eurent, comme veoye,
A plaisir et a gré le vent.

Mon cueur, Penser et moy, nous troys,
Les regardasmes a grant joye,
Et dit mon cueur a basse vois,
'Voulentiers en ce point feroye,
De Confort la voile tendroye,
Se je cuidoye seurement
Avoir, ainsi que je vouldroye,
A plaisir et a gré le vent.

'Mais je treuve le plus des mois
L'eaue de Fortune si quoye,
Quant ou bateau du Monde vois,
Que, s'avirons d'Espoir n'avoye,
Souvent en chemin demouroye,
En trop grant ennuy longuement;
Pour neant en vain actendroye
A plaisir et a gré le vent.'

Si rencontré, and I met.
singloient, were sailing.
comme veoye, as I could see.
Se je cuidoye seurement avoir, if I could rely on having.
quoye, still.
vois, I travel.
avirons, oars.
demouroye, I should stay.

Les nefz dont cy devant parloye
Montoient, et je descendoye
Contre les vagues de Tourment;
Quant il lui plaira, Dieu m'envoye
A plaisir et a gré le vent.

nefz, ships.

This is followed by the ballade on the recovery of Guyenne and
Normandy by the French, by various playful poems using legal
vocabulary, and by others in macaronics (example, 'Prince, miscui
en potage/Latinum et françois langage . . .') by the Duke and
friends.

En la forest de Longue Actente,
Chevauchant par divers sentiers
M'en voys, ceste annee presente,
Ou voyage de Desiriers.
Devant sont allez mes fourriers
Pour appareiller mon logis
En la cité de Destinee;
Et pour mon cueur et moy ont pris
L'ostellerie de Pensee.

Je mayne des chevaulx quarente
Et autant pour mes officiers,
Voire, par Dieu, plus de soixante,
Sans les bagaiges et sommiers.
Loger nous fauldra par quartiers,
Se les hostelz sont trop petis;
Toutesfoiz, pour une vespree,
En gré prendray, soit mieulx ou pis,
L'ostellerie de Pensee.

Je despens chascun jour ma rente
En maintz travaulx avanturiers,
Dont est Fortune mal contente
Qui soutient contre moy Dangiers;
Mais Espoirs, s'ilz sont droicturiers
Et tiennent ce qu'ilz m'ont promis,
Je pense faire telle armée
Qu'auray, malgré mes ennemis,
L'ostellerie de Pensee.

Prince, vray Dieu de paradis,
Vostre grace me soit donnee,
Telle que treuve, a mon devis,
L'ostellerie de Pensee.

In the forest of Long Awaiting,
Riding by different pathways
I set out in this present year
On the journey of Desire.
My *fourriers* have gone on before
To prepare my lodging
In the city of Destiny;
And they have taken for my heart and myself
The hostelry of Thought.

I bring with me forty horse
And as many for the officers of my household,
Indeed, by God, more than sixty,
Without the baggage animals and beasts of burden.
We shall have to be billeted about the town,
If the lodging houses are too small;
Yet for one evening
I shall accept gladly, for better or worse,
The hostelry of Thought.

I spend my allowance every day
In many casual expenses,
Which displease Fortune
Who supports Dangier against me;
But if Hopes are righteous
And keep the promises they made me
I trust to have such an army
That I shall hold, despite my enemies,
The hostelry of Thought.

Prince, true God of Paradise,
Thy grace be given me
That I may find, to my desire,
The hostelry of Thought.

This line-by-line crib shows how very difficult it is to capture the poetry of the French words. Remember that *fourriers* are servants sent on ahead to prepare and if necessary requisition lodging for an important person travelling from town to town—cf. Summer's *fourriers* in rondeau XXX—and that *Pensee* is only very inadequately translated by modern English 'thought'—see Introduction.

After this, come further ballades and a collection of pieces by other hands, including Villon's poem(s) *'O louee concepcion'* and *'Combien que j'ay leu en ung dit'* (probably not in Villon's autograph but perhaps copied from it by someone else) on the birth (or triumphal entry into Orléans) of Charles' daughter Marie in 1457 (or 1460), and the poems entered for the 'Débat de la fontaine', a competition involving Villon, Montbeton, maistre Berthault de Villebresme, Charles' doctor Caillau, and many others.

There follows a group of *chansons*, 85 in French, two macaronic in French and Latin, and two in English.

Se ma doleur vous saviés,
Mon seul joyeux pensement,
Je sçay bien certainement
Que mercy de moy auriés.

Du tout Refus banniriés
Qui me tient en ce tourment,
Se ma [doleur vous saviés,]
Mon seul [joyeux pensement.]

Et le don me donneriés
Que vous ay requis souvent,
Pour avoir allegement;
Ja ne m'en escondiriés,
Se ma [doleur vous saviés.]

escondiriés, you would dismiss.

In one of the English songs, the line 'In blake mournyng is clothyd my corage' certainly suggests Charles' own *'Je suis cellui cueur vestu de noir'*. Champion prints in the notes (pp. 569ff.) the other pieces in English found in this MS, and two French fragments said to be by Charles and preserved in MS Harley 7333.

Next are grouped five *complaintes*; I give excerpts from the first, written during Charles' imprisonment, perhaps in 1433.

France, jadis on te souloit nommer,
En tous pays, le tresor de noblesse,
Car un chascun povoit en toy trouver
Bonté, honneur, loyauté, gentillesse,
Clergie, sens, courtoisie, proesse.
Tous estrangiers amoient te suir;
Et maintenant voy, dont j'ay desplaisance,
Qu'il te couvient maint grief mal soustenir,
Trescrestien, franc royaume de France!

Scez tu dont vient ton mal, a vray parler?
Congnois tu point pourquoy es en tristesse?
Conter le vueil, pour vers toy m'acquiter,
Escoutes moy et tu feras sagesse.
Ton grant ourgueil, glotonnie, peresse,
Couvoitise, sans justice tenir,
Et luxure, dont as eu abondance,
Ont pourchacié vers Dieu de te punir,
Trescretien, franc royaume de France!

Ne te vueilles pour tant desesperer,
Car Dieu est plain de merci, a largesse.
Va t'en vers lui sa grace demander,
Car il t'a fait, deja pieça, promesse
(Mais que faces ton advocat Humblesse)
Que tresjoyeux sera de toy guerir;
Entierement metz en lui ta fiance,
Pour toy et tous, voulu en crois mourir,
Trescretien, franc royaume de France!

Note that *Trescrestien* is an official title of the French King.

France, in time past men used to call you
In every land the treasure of nobleness,
For every one might find in you
Goodness, honour, loyalty, noble behaviour,
Learning, wit, courtesy, prowess.
All foreigners loved to follow you;
And now I see, which saddens me,
That you must suffer many a painful hurt,
Most Christian, freeborn realm of France!

Do you know whence comes your ill, to tell the truth?
Know you not why you are in misery?
I will tell, in order to do my duty to you,
Listen to me and you will act wisely.
Your great pride, gluttony and sloth,
Covetousness that has no regard for justice,
And luxury (lechery) in which you have abounded
Have caused God to punish you,
Most Christian, freeborn realm of France!

Yet for that do not despair,
For God is full of mercy and gives it freely.
Approach him to ask his grace,
For already long ago he promised you
That if you would make Humility your advocate
He would be most delighted to cure you;
Put your trust wholly in him;
For you and for all he was willing to die on the cross,
Most Christian, freeborn realm of France!

. . . Quelz champions souloit en toy trouver
Crestienté! Ja ne fault que l'expresse;
Charlemeine, Rolant et Olivier
En sont tesmoings; pour ce, je m'en delaisse.
Et saint Loys Roy, qui fist la rudesse
Des Sarrasins souvent aneantir,
En son vivant, par travail et vaillance!
Les croniques le moustrent, sans mentir,
Trescrestien, franc royaume de France!

. . . Dieu a les bras ouvers pour t'acoler,
Prest d'oublier ta vie pecheresse;
Requier pardon, bien te vendra aidier
Nostre Dame, la trespuissant princesse,
Qui est ton cry et que tiens pour maistresse.
Les sains aussi te vendront secourir,
Desquelz les corps font en toy demourance.
Ne vueilles plus en ton pechié dormir,
Trescrestien, franc royaume de France!

Et je, Charles, duc d'Orleans, rimer
Voulu ces vers ou temps de ma jeunesse,
Devant chascun les vueil bien advouer,
Car prisonnier les fis, je le confesse;
Priant a Dieu, qu'avant qu'aye vieillesse,
Le temps de paix partout puist avenir,
Comme de cueur j'en ay la desirance,
Et que voye tous tes maulx brief finir,
Trescrestien, franc royaume de France!

... What champions Christianity used to find in you!
I need not expound this at length;
Charlemagne, Roland and Oliver are
Witnesses of this, so I say no more.
And Saint Louis the King, that often
Destroyed the cruelty of the Saracens
In his lifetime, by hard toil and valiance!
The chronicles tell us this, without a lie,
Most Christian, freeborn realm of France!

... God holds his arms open to embrace you,
Ready to forget your sinful life;
Ask forgiveness, Our Lady,
That most powerful princess, will come to your aid,
She who is your battle cry and whom you honour as mistress.
The saints too will come to help you
Whose bodies rest in you;
Sleep no more in your sin,
Most Christian, freeborn realm of France!

And I, Charles, Duke of Orléans,
Have wished to write these verses in the time of my youth;
I shall admit it before everyone,
For I made them while in prison, I confess,
Praying God, that before I am old
The time of peace may everywhere have come,
As I heartily desire,
And that I may soon see an end to all your woes,
Most Christian, freeborn realm of France!

There are four *caroles*, one in Latin and three in French, then follow 435 *rondeaux*, many by Charles, others answering or provoking poems of his, by Charles de Nevers, King René d'Anjou (author of the *Livre du Cuer d'amours esprins*), by Charles' son-in-law the duc d'Alençon, Maître Caillau, Benoît Damien, the duc de Bourbon, and indeed by any passing or resident poets connected with the court of Blois. I select a handful of these pieces, and refer the reader desirous of more to the collections of Bernard and Tardieu, or to Champion's complete edition.

Rondeau XIX; Champion p. 301, MS p. 350. Autograph

> Maistre Estienne Le Gout, nominatif,
> Nouvellement, par maniere optative,
> Si a voulu faire copulative;
> Mais failli a en son cas genitif.
>
> Il avoit mis .vj. ducatz en datif,
> Pour mielx avoir s'amie vocative,
> Maistre Estienne [Le Gout, nominatif.]
>
> Quant rencontré a un acusatif
> Qui sa robe lui a fait ablative;
> De fenestre assez superlative
> A fait un sault portant coups en passif,
> Maistre Estienne [Le Gout, nominatif.]

This is followed by Le Gout's reply in similar terminology, '*Monseigneur, tressupellatif*', rather weak but doing his best to keep up the game. This playing with technical grammatical (or in some cases legal) terms was a favourite type of pleasantry.

Les fourriers d'Esté sont venus
Pour appareillier son logis,
Et ont fait tendre ses tappis,
De fleurs et verdure tissus.

En estandant tappis velus,
De verte herbe par le païs,
Les fourriers [d'Esté sont venus.]

Cueurs d'ennuy pieça morfondus,
Dieu mercy, sont sains et jolis;
Alez vous ent, prenez païs,
Yver, vous ne demourrés plus;
Les fourriers [d'Esté sont venus.]

fourriers, servants who went ahead of a feudal progress to find and prepare accommodation for the lord and his company.
Esté, Summer.
pieça, for a long time.
morfondus, sunk, overwhelmed (in melancholy).
demourrés, will stay.

Rondeau XXXI; Champion p. 307, MS p. 365. Lines 5–13 are in Charles' own hand, and he has added *brouderie* in 1.3, and *luyant* for *rayant* in 1.4

> Le temps a laissié son manteau
> De vent, de froidure et de pluye,
> Et s'est vestu de brouderie,
> De soleil luyant, cler et beau.
>
> Il n'y a beste ne oyseau
> Qu'en son jargon ne chante ou crie,
> Le temps [a laissié son manteau!]
>
> Riviere, fontaine et ruisseau
> Portent, en livree jolie,
> Gouttes d'argent d'orfaverie,
> Chascun s'abille de nouveau;
> Le temps [a laissié son manteau.]

orfaverie, goldsmiths' or jewellers' work.

This anonymous translation appeared in the *London Magazine* for Sept. 1823: 'The Time hath laid his mantle by/Of wind and rain and icy chill,/And dons a rich embroidery/Of sun-light pour'd on lake and hill.//No beast or bird in earth or sky/Whose voice doth not with gladness thrill,/For Time hath laid his mantle by/Of wind and rain and icy chill.//River and fountain, brook and rill,/Bespangled o'er with livery gay,/Of silver droplets, wind their way:/So all their new apparel vie;/The Time hath laid his mantle by.' While not completely accurate, it succeeds in conveying much of the original's flavour.

Dedens mon livre de Pensee
J'ay trouvé escripvant mon cueur
La vraye histoire de douleur,
De larmes toute enluminee,

En deffassant la tresamee
Ymage de plaisant doulceur,
Dedens [mon livre de Pensee.]

Helas! ou l'a mon cueur trouvee?
Lez grossez gouttez de sueur
Lui saillent, de peinne et labeur
Qu'il y prent, et nuit et journee,
Dedens [mon livre de Pensee.]

enluminee, illuminated.
tresamee, much beloved.
Lui saillent, pour from him.

En regardant ces belles fleurs
Que le temps nouveau d'Amours prie,
Chascune d'elles s'ajolie
Et farde de plaisans couleurs.

Tant enbasmees sont de odeurs
Qu'il n'est cueur qui ne rajeunie,
En regardant [ces belles fleurs.]

Lez oyseaus deviennent danseurs
Dessuz mainte branche flourie,
Et font joyeuse chanterie,
De contres, deschans et teneurs,
En regardant [ces belles fleurs.]

enbasmees, perfumed.
mainte, many a.

Quant commanceray a voler,
Et sur elles me sentiray,
En si grant aise je seray
Que j'ay doubte de m'essorer.

Beau crier aura et leurrer,
Chemin de Plaisant Vent tendray,
Quant [commanceray a voler,
Et sur elles me sentiray.]

La mue m'a fallu garder
Par long temps; plus ne le feray,
Puis que doulx temps et cler verray;
On le me devra pardonner,
Quant [commanceray a voler.]

elles, wings, *m'essorer*, soar away.
Line 5 means 'Shouting and waving the lure will be in vain';
d'Héricault gives *Beau Crier aura le levrier*, which does not seem to
make much sense.
La mue, cage where the falcon is confined when losing feathers.

Ce premier jour du mois de May,
Quant de mon lit hors me levay,
Environ vers la matinee
Dedans mon jardin de Pensee
Avecques mon cueur seul entray.

Dieu scet s'entrepris fu d'esmay,
Car en pleurant tout regarday
Destruit d'ennuyeuse gelee,
Ce premier ⌈jour du mois de May,
Quant de mon lit hors me levay,
Environ vers la matinee.⌉

En gast, fleurs et arbres trouvay;
Lors au jardinier demanday
Se Desplaisance maleuree,
Par tempeste, vent ou nuee,
Avoit fait tel piteux array,
Ce premier ⌈jour du mois de May.⌉

entrepris, overcome.
en gast, ruined, laid waste.
maleuree, accursed.
Avoit is from d'Héricault's edition; Champion misprints *avoir*.

Temps et temps m'on⁺ emblé Jennesse,
Et laissé es mains de Viellesse
Ou vois mon pouvre pain querant;
Aage ne me veult, tant ne quant,
Donner l'aumosne de Liesse.

Puis qu'elle se tient ma maistresse,
Demander ne luy puis promesse,
Pour ce, n'enquerons plus avant.
Temps [et temps m'ont emblé Jennesse,
Et laissé es mains de Viellesse.]

Je n'ay repast que de Foiblesse,
Couchant sur paille de Destresse,
Suy je bien payé maintenant
De mes jennes jours cy devant?
Nennil, nul n'est qui le redresse;
Temps et temps [m'ont emblé Jennesse.]

Time and times have stolen Youth from me,
And left me in the hands of Old Age
Where I go begging my poor bread;
Age will not give me even a scrap
Of the alms of Joy.

Since she (Age) considers herself my mistress,
I cannot ask any promise of her.
And so, let us not seek any further.
Time and times have stolen Youth from me,
And left me in the hands of Old Age.

I have no food but Weakness,
I sleep on the straw of Destitution.
Am I well paid now
For my young days in time past?
Indeed not, there is no-one to redress my wrong;
Time and times have stolen Youth from me.

Salués moy toute la compaignie
Ou a present estez a chiere lye,
Et leur dites que voluentiés seroye
Avecques eulx, mais estre n'y pourroye,
Pour Viellesse qui m'a en sa ballie.

Au temps passé, Jennesse sy jolie
Me gouvernoit; las! or n'y suy ge mie,
Et pour cela, pour Dieu, que escuzé soye;
Salués [moy toute la compaignie
Ou a present estez a chiere lye.]

Amoureus fus, or ne le suy ge mye,
Et en Paris menoye bonne vie;
Adieu bon temps, ravoir ne vous saroye!
Bien sanglé fus d'une estrete courroye,
Que, par Age, convient que la deslie;
Salués moy toute la compaignie!

a chiere lye, with happy expressions, with good cheer.
que escuzé soye, let me be excused.
or ne le suy ge mie, now I am not at all.
saroye, could not, would not know how to.
sanglé, girded.
courroye, strap, harness, belt.

The mede is flowe the grace is goon
The hert is chaungid from his place
Where y had wende hem be he nas
Thus myrthe and y are comen foon
But fy allas that a wise oon
Shulde hay/or thay se what to chas
       The mede is
       The hert is
Yet trust y lo to fynde aloon
An hert if that y haue the grace
And if y onys may that purchace
Then hay on hardely euerichoon
       The mede is
       The hert is

comen foon, become enemies.
Punning on hart/heart and on mede (meadow, or reward) reminiscent of early Tudor poetry, of Wyatt perhaps.

My gostly fadir y me confesse
First to god and then to yow
That at a window wot ye how
I stale a cosse of gret swetnes
Which done was out avisynes
But hit is doon not vndoon now
       My gostly
       First to
But y restore it shalle dowtles
Ageyn if so be that y mow
And that [to] god y make a vow
And ellis y axe foryefnes
       My gostly
       First to

cosse, kiss.
out avisynes, without thinking.

The smylyng mouth and laughyng eyen gray
The brestis rounde and long smal armys twayne
The hondis smothe the sidis streiyt & playne
Yowre fetis lite what shulde y ferther say
Hit is my craft when ye are fer away
To muse theron in styntyng of my payne
        The smylyng
        The brestis
So wolde y pray yow gef y durste or may
The sight to se as y haue seyne
Forwhi that craft me is most fayne
And wol ben to the howre in which y day
        The smylyng
        The brestis

Aftir wyntir the veer with foylis grene
Aftir the sterry nyght the morow gray
Lucyna chaungyng in her hornys shene
The enpese made of many gret affray
The sondry chaunge of thingis se y may
But ye swet hert so voyde are of pite
That for no thyng y kan yow write or say
The chaunge of yowre mystrust kan y not se

Both fowle and best with word entamyd bene
The spirit also with speche enforsid say
The trouthe of thing that man wol litille wene
With speche the heven to perse this is no nay
But what promys or oth y make ma fay

foylis, leaves.
enpese, peace, S.
ma fay, mild asseveration, 'by my faith'.

As in no wise can y entristid be
So to vntrewe ye thynke me welaway
The chaunge of yowre mystrust kan y not see

But though that ye me throwe thus in ruyne
It in me shalle be founde to that y day
Mi trouth as fresshely newe forto be sene
As y it had bigonne yestirday
But and it myght like yow to putt away
Yowre daunger and mystrust that grevith me
I shulde be bound to yow for onys and ay
That cause me to mystrust ye shal not se

Though that my wordis be not ovir gay
They ben y-seid with as trew fantase
As thei say whiche make more fresshe aray
The chaunge of yowre mystrust if y myght se

to that y day, until I die.

Steele p. 195; no French equivalent

Welcome my ioy welcome myn hertis ese
Welcome my lady welcome my plesaunce
Welcome my sovl comfort in alle disese
Welcome enlesser of my gret grevaunce
Welcome of ricchesse myn hool suffisaunce
Welcome the heuene y most desire to haue
Welcome whiche haue my lijf in gouernaunce
Welcome my leche me forto sle or saue

Right as your absence was to me an hele
Right so your presence is to me a blis
Even as the sight of yow me gevith wele
Even so y payne when sight of yow y mys
A thousand sithe y wisshid haue or this

enlesser, lessener.

A thowsand sythe on row that ye were arave
But welcome now to mende that is a-mys
And welcome now my leche to sle or saue

Now good swet hert as this remembre yow
How longe a-part we were thorugh infortune
Now good swet hert wherfore bithynke as how
How longe we mowe as in this ioy contune
For alle in yow hit lith as my fortune
Welcome what ye me geve y not disprave
For alle my myrthe ye mate may or entewne
Welcome no more but now me sle or saue

What may y more yow write at wordis fewe
The ioy of yow welnygh me doth raue
Welcome as oft as tonge kan say on rewe
Welcome no more but now me sle or saue

arave, arrived.
contune, continue, S.
disprave, disparage, S.
mate or entewne, bring to nothing or bring into harmony, S.

Steele, rondel 60

Fare wel fare wel my lady and maystres
Fare wel that y most loue and evir shalle
Fare wel allas hit shulde me thus bifalle
Fare wel the hope of my ioy and gladnes
Not may y speke for payne and hevynes
And yowre departyng is the cause of alle
      Fare wel
      Fare wel
For vnto waylyng wepyng and distres
From this tyme forth bicomen must y thral
Syn that y may not stroke the sidis smal
Of yowre swete body ful of lustynes
      Fare wel
      Fare wel

BIBLIOGRAPHY

1) Pierre Champion, *Vie de Charles d'Orléans* (Honoré Champion, Paris, 1911).

2) Ibid., *Le manuscrit autographe des poésies de Charles d'Orléans* (Ibid., 1907).

3) *The English Poems of Charles of Orleans*, edited from B.M. M.S. Harl. 682, by Robert Steele (E.E.T.S., O.U.P., 1941).

4) *The English Poems of Charles d'Orléans*, vol. II, Notes, by Robert Steele and Mabel Day (E.E.T.S., O.U.P., 1946).

5) 3 & 4 reprinted in one volume, 1970.

6) John Fox, *The Lyric Poetry of Charles d'Orléans* (O.U.P., 1969).

7) Aimé Champollion-Figeac, *Les Poésies du duc Charles d'Orléans* (Paris, 1842). 'Première édition complète de ses ouvrages.'

8) Jacques Choffel, *Le Duc Charles d'Orléans* (Debresse, Paris, 1968).

9) Jean Tardieu, *Charles d'Orléans, choix de rondeaux* (Egloff, Paris, 1947).

10) Jacques Charpier, *Charles d'Orléans* (Ecrivains d'hier et d'aujourd'hui, Paris, 1958). Pretentious and unsympathetic.

11) Constant Beaufils, *Étude sur la vie et es poésies de Charles d'Orléans* (Coutances, 1861).

12) Robert Louis Stevenson, *Familiar Studies of Men and Books* (Chatto & Windus, London, 1923). Damns with damnably faint praise.

13) (P. V. Chalvet), *Poésies de Charles d'Orléans, Père de Louis XII et Oncle de François Ier, Rois de France* (B. Warée, Paris, 1809). Hopes to restore the poet to his due eminence by this 'choix de Poësies qui parait pour la premiere fois'.

14) Nigel Wilkins, *One Hundred Ballades, Rondeaux and Virelais from the later Middle Ages* (C.U.P., 1969).

15) Cedric Wallis, *Charles d'Orléans and other French poets, Rondels* (Caravel Press, London, 1951). Limited edition of 150. Contains text and version of 13 pieces by Charles.

16) Pierre Champion, *Charles d'Orléans, Poésies* (Honoré Champion, Paris, 1923-7).

17) Georg Bullrich, *Über Charles d'Orléans und die ihm zugeschriebene englische Übersetzung seiner Gedichte* (Berlin, 1893). 24 pp.

18) *Studi Francesi*, 1959, fasc. I, art. Gilbert Ouy. Examines a long Latin poem in monorhymed quatrains, mystic and devotional in content, *Canticum Amoris*, written after the death of Charles' second wife c.1435.

19) Dr. Ethel Seaton, *Studies in Villon, Vaillant and Charles d'Orléans* (Blackwell, Oxford, 1957). Remarkable Baconian piece about anagrams and acrostics.

20) Jean-Marc Bernard, *Œuvres II* (Le Divan, Paris, 1923). Short essay on Charles, preface to a selection of his rondeaux.

21) William Shakespeare, *King Henry V*, ed. J. H. Walter (Methuen, London, 1954).

22) Charles d'Héricault, *Poésies Complètes de Charles d'Orléans* (Alphonse Lemerre, Paris, 1874). 2 vols.

23) *Comptes Rendus de l'Académie des Inscriptions*, 1955, paper read by Gilbert Ouy, 'Recherches sur la librairie de Charles d'Orléans et de Jean d'Angoulême pendant leur captivité en Angleterre, et étude de deux manuscrits autographes de Charles d'Orléans récemment identifiés'.

24) George Watson Taylor, *Poems, written in English, by Charles Duke of Orleans, during his captivity in England after the battle of Azincourt* (Shakespeare Press, London, 1827). Limited edition for the Roxburghe Club. 'Now first printed from the manuscript in the library of the British Museum', Harleian 682.

25) *Romania* 49, 1923, art. Pierre Champion, 'A propos de Charles d'Orléans'.

26) (Albert Pauphilet), *Poésies de Charles d'Orléans* (Le Livre Français, Paris, 1926).

27) *Annales Poétiques, ou Almanach des Muses, Depuis l'origine de la Poésie Françoise*, Tome I (Delalain, Paris, 1788). Essay and 25 poems; reasonably good text.

28) Ferdinand Kuhl, *Die Allegorie bei Charles d'Orléans* (Marburg, 1886). Useful and thorough list of Charles' personifications and 'materialisations'.

29) *Mémoires/ de Littérature,/ tirez des registres/ de l'Académie Royale/ des Inscriptions/ et Belles Lettres*, Tome 13, 1740, paper read by M. l'Abbé Sallier, 'Observations sur un recueil manuscrit de poesies de Charles d'Orléans', on 21 Jan. 1734. Discusses the present B.N. fr. 1104; analyses the first poems and examines their style.

30) *The Retrospective Review, and Historical and Antiquarian Magazine*, Second Series, vol. I (London, 1827), review of Watson Taylor, pp. 147ff. Concludes that Harl. 682 cannot possibly be by Charles at all.

31) *Mélanges offerts à M. Émile Picot*, vol. I (Paris, 1913). Article by Pierre Champion, 'Du succès de l'oeuvre de Charles d'Orléans et de ses imitateurs jusqu' au XVIe siècle'.

32) Wilhelm König, *Zur Französischen Literaturgeschichte Studien und Skizzen* (Halle, 1877).

33) N. L. Goodrich, *Charles of Orléans, A Study of Themes in his French and in his English Poetry* (Genève, 1967). Intelligent introduction, the best part of the book.

34) M. l'Abbé Goujet, *Bibliothèque Françoise*, Tome IX (Paris, 1745). Admits Charles as an English author, and points out late fifteenth- and early sixteenth-century plagiarisms of his work in early printed anthologies.

35) *Publications of the Modern Language Association of America*, 1911, art. Henry Noble MacCracken, 'An English Friend of Charles of Orléans'. Suggests that the English poems in the Royal M.S. and in B. N. fr. 25458 are by William de la Pole, Duke of Suffolk.

36) *The Gentleman's Magazine*, May 1842, art. 'The English Poems of Charles Duke of Orleans'. Supports Watson Taylor against Sir Thomas Croft, the reviewer in the *Retrospective Review*, and feels it 'most probable' that the originals of all the English poems exist in the M.S. in the Bibliothèque du Roi, mentioned by Sallier.

37) *Romania* 21, 1892, art. A. Piaget, 'Une édition gothique de Charles d'Orléans'.

38) *Romania* 22, 1893, art. A. Thomas, 'Les premiers vers de Charles d'Orléans,' discusses the *Livre contre tout péché* that Charles wrote when he was ten.

39) *Romania* 86, 1965, art. John Fox, 'Charles d'Orléans, poète anglais ?'

40) Pierre Champion, *La Librairie de Charles d'Orléans* (Honoré Champion, Paris, 1910). Fascinating, excellent.

41) Sergio Cigada, *L'Opera Poetica di Charles d'Orléans* (Milano, 1960). Clear and concise; hair-raising amount of bibliography. Believes the English translations to have been made by an unknown contemporary.

42) *Revue Historique*, Sept.–Oct. 1896, art. Gustave Dupont-Ferrier, 'La Captivité de Jean d'Orléans, Comte d'Angoulême'. Demonstrates the abominable rapacity and bad faith of the brothers' English gaolers admirably.

43) *The London Magazine*, Sept. 1823, art. 'Charles, Duke of Orleans'. Gives five translations from the 1809 edition and a biographical sketch full of mistakes.

44) *Le Moyen Age* XLIX, 1939, art. Marius Barroux, 'La Forme des Rondeaux et Chansons de Charles d'Orléans'.

45) *Revue d'Histoire Diplomatique* XVIII, 1904, art, Léon Mirot,

'Isabelle de France, Reine d'Angleterre, Comtesse d'Angoulême, Duchesse d'Orléans'.

46) Ditto, 1905, continuation of the above.

47) *Anglia* XVII, 1895, art. Emil Hausknecht, 'Vier Gedichte von Charles d'Orléans', deals with the Bodleian Hearne Fragment (Hearne's Diaries, 38, pp. 261–4), two leaves from a parchment M.S. of *c.*1440. Prints the songs and identifies them in Watson Taylor.

48) *Modern Language Notes* LXVI, 1951, art. Russell Hope Robbins, 'Some Charles d'Orléans Fragments'. Prints text of two detached vellum leaves in C.U.L., Additional 2585, belonging to the same volume as the Hearne Fragment and copied like it from the Harley M.S.

49) *Bulletin du Bibliophile*, March 1923, art. A. Perreau, 'La Véritable Édition Originale des Poésies de Charles d'Orléans', describes 'une sorte de tirage à part' from the *Almanach des Muses* of 1778—probably a very limited edition.

50) *Reliquiae Hearnianae*, ed. Philip Bliss, vol. I (Oxford, 1857). Prints 'exactly from the originals' the 'Four old Love Songs, I know not who the author' above mentioned.

51) E. Droz and J. Thibault, *Poètes et Musiciens du XVe siècle* (Paris, 1924). Music of *Je ne prise point tels baysiers* and *Va tost mon amoreux desir*, composer unknown, from Escorial IV a. 24 and B.N. fr. 15123.

52) *The Romanic Review* LVI, 1965, art. Harold Watson, O.S.B., 'Charles d'Orléans: 1394–1465'. Examines themes of Love and Nonchaloir,